POSITIVELY

PAZZO

Learning Italian and Travels in Italy

a memoir

MICHAEL FRANCIS

DISCLAIMER

I have tried to recreate events, locales, and conversations from my memories of them. In order to maintain anonymity, in some instances I have changed the names of individuals and places. I may have changed some identifying characteristics and details such as physical properties, occupations, and places of residence.

This book is dedicated to my
friend and classmate Pam McMillan.

Contents

PART ONE

Back to School

Chapter 1

Before We Begin

If my friend Emily had a credit card, I might never have written this book.

Emily still uses a check book and refuses to believe it isn't 1974 anymore.

A talented pastel artist who lives in Williamsburg, Brooklyn, she had wanted to learn Italian for several years before she came across an Italian for Beginners course at a Lifelong Learning Institute.

Having successfully enrolled in a class via the school's website, she was obliged to pay a modest tuition fee.

That's where I come in.

Not for the first time, I was asked to produce a credit card and pay the outstanding amount on her behalf.

I would later be reimbursed in cash and rewarded for my trouble, more often than not with a packet of chocolate chip cookies.

Suffice it to say, it was a pretty good deal.

When she rang and asked me to pay the bill, I was curious to know what it was for.

"I want to learn Italian," she said. "There's a Beginners' Course at the Lifelong Learning Institute in Brooklyn. It starts in September."

Four years of French at school, more than forty years ago, clearly hadn't satisfied my thirst for language learning, and almost as a reflex, I replied, "What a great idea! I'll come and do it with you."

Of course, it would have been entirely appropriate and terribly clever to preface my response with words such as 'brava' or 'ottima,' but at this stage, I couldn't be sure what those words actually meant.

Some fifteen years before, I had spent ten days in Italy with a handful of friends and had a wonderful time, even though none of us could speak or understand a single word of the language.

All the same, I had long considered Italian 'una lingua bellissima.' It has a delightfully lyrical, almost poetic quality, to say nothing of an intrinsic association with the country's wonderful food, wine, and unique culture.

Anyway, for sixty bucks a year, what did I have to lose?

I studied the enrollment criteria for the Lifelong Learning Institute, to discover that the school was essentially the domain of the retiree, or at the very least, those who consider themselves 'semi-retired.'

At the time, I had just celebrated a birthday that, strictly speaking, marked me a good ten years short of a recognized retirement age. Even so, I concluded that carving out a living as an author met with at least most of the qualifying criteria listed on the website.

After all, it's not like I had a real job.

It soon became apparent that Italian for Beginners was just one of the many and varied opportunities the LLI presented.

In fact, the school offered its members a plethora of educational opportunities, a veritable A to Z of classes, with courses in Art to Zen Meditation.

I carefully scrolled through a long list on the website that detailed everything from knitting for novices to puppet-making, Spanish, and Bridge. I raced past an entire section on Cryptic Crosswords, which offered lessons for the confused to the advanced, with one specific module rather appropriately defined as 'Self Help.'

I eventually found Italian for Beginners and discovered that the course would be presented in the school's art room every Monday between 11:30 am and 1:30 pm. The course was listed as open for enrollment, and the teacher was a woman named Bronwyn Street.

A brief period of social media research followed.

I discovered that Bronwyn Street was a very genial and attractive woman who lived in Greenpoint. She seemed to keep herself busy by entertaining any number of grandchildren, when not sipping coffee, strolling in the park, or teaching Italian, presumably.

I enrolled in the course and paid our respective annual fees, after which Emily and I were each allocated a four-digit member identification number.

We were in.

Italian school would start on Monday next week, and I could look forward to devouring a packet of chocolate chip cookies in the meantime.

Life was good.

Chapter 2

First Day of School

I collected Emily from her apartment at 11:00 am, and we traveled to class together.

I drove while she navigated.

From the moment we arrived, it was clear that the school was a popular endeavor.

A parking lot that wound its way around various buildings, housed fifty vehicles, with a dozen more cars lining the street outside.

Happily, our arrival seemed to coincide with the conclusion of the morning's earlier classes, and after hovering patiently for a few seconds, we secured a parking space.

Our first order of business was to register with a couple of volunteers who had set up camp behind a folding table just outside the office.

These people checked us in, handing us each a printed name tag that was inserted into a clear plastic sleeve and suspended from a cloth lanyard.

The tags displayed our name and membership number, together with the name and telephone number of the person we had previously specified as an emergency contact on the reverse.

Emily and I dutifully donned our tags before making our way into the main building.

To the right was a French class in Meeting Rooms 1 and 2. Beyond that was the kitchen, and straight ahead to the left, was the art room and Italian for Beginners.

I held the door open for Emily, who, having recognized a friend seated inside darted across the room, before I wandered in carrying a notebook and pen. I nodded hello to ten fellow students, all reposing at tables neatly arranged in a horseshoe in front of a free-standing whiteboard, a small folding table, and a single chair.

A couple of glass doors at the back of the room presented a view of a timber fence, beyond which was a childcare center. A front corner housed two sturdy concrete sinks, each liberally adorned with generations of paint, while a clock on the wall confirmed the time to be 11:25 am.

Most of the chairs in the room consisted of a flimsy molded plastic attached to a lightweight metal frame. They were cheap, stackable, and just the sort of thing I was likely to snap in two should I lean back while mulling over a tricky translation.

However, there were a couple of sturdier constructs resting in the corner. I wandered over, liberated one, and sat at one end of the back row facing the teacher's desk.

A robust timber pole stood a few yards to my left. It was more or less in the middle of the room, just in front of a row of tables and doubtless holding up the ceiling. It had a six-inch diameter, which may prove just enough of a barrier to avoid the teacher's gaze should she be searching for a student to deal with a particularly curly question.

Sadly, someone had already secured that spot.

Instead, I sat next to a woman named Susan, while she in turn was seated next to Deborah.

Susan and Deborah knew each other quite well, and after chatting briefly with them both, I discovered that they had enrolled in what was effectively the same course the previous year.

Susan because she had a general interest in the language, and Deborah because she stayed in Italy for a few weeks each year (always in the same small village) and she felt it was about time that she could engage in a few simple conversations with the locals.

Their class started with fifteen students and dwindled to eight after just three weeks. Halfway through its second semester, Deborah was the only student left, and only then because she was flying to Rome in a few weeks.

Unfortunately, their instructor proved to be a graduate of the Benito Mussolini Teachers' College and Charm School.

From all reports, she was a very aggressive individual who all but demanded answers from her students, while savagely criticizing any of their colleagues who dared to help.

She would hover over her victims menacingly, insisting they knew the answer to her questions, and fiercely reminding anyone who tried to help, that she was the teacher, not them!

I thought it was a great credit to them both that they bothered to show up a second time.

Just after the two women had shared their experience with me, our clearly very different teacher entered the room.

Cheerful, smiling, and slender, she wore spectacles and sported straight, shoulder-length, silvery-grey hair.

She was carrying a three-ring binder, a plastic container of whiteboard markers, and the biggest dictionary I had ever seen. It looked like a foundation stone from the Coliseum, wrapped in a bright green dust jacket.

I can remember thinking, "If the Italian language has that many words, variations, exceptions, and verb conjugations, I may as well pack it in here and now."

Our teacher introduced herself and confirmed her name on the whiteboard, writing Bronwyn Street, before translating her last name (in brackets) to 'Strada.'

With the binder lying open on her desk, she took the roll, asking each of us to explain who we were, where we lived, and what, if any, experience we had with the Italian language.

Throughout the process, our names were Italianized when possible.

I became Michele, and needless to say, Emily was anointed Emilia. My neighbor became Susanna, and Stefano was a little further to her left. He was the one who had the sense to sit behind the pole. Giuliana, Giovanni, and Elena sat around the corner to his left, and Roberto was across the room.

Sadly, there wasn't much we could do with Graham, Deborah, Barbara, Wendy, and two Kayes.

Bronwyn explained the structure of the course and that she was 'la professoressa.' A rather grand title that in Italy is bestowed upon female secondary school teachers, as readily as those who have in fact secured a PhD.

We were introduced to the textbook we should all acquire, as it was the volume we would be working through during the year.

I was half expecting 'Italian for Dummies,' but the book was called 'Italian De-Mystified.' It was written by some bloke who actually did have a PhD., and the cover featured a rather sporty illustration of a woman riding a Vespa.

The book, a premium third edition, no less, was linked to the publisher's website, where we could access various videos, recordings, and exercises online.

Italian De-Mystified promised to 'Untangle Complicated Grammar Rules,' allowing us to 'Master Essential Italian Verb Tenses.'

As if that wasn't enough, we could 'Build a Rich Italian Vocabulary,' while 'Reinforcing our Skills with Quizzes, Oral Exercises, and, God forbid, a Final Exam.'

Some of us already owned the book, but most would need to order one from a local bookshop or buy a copy online.

That'll be another packet of chocolate chip cookies for me then.

In the absence of a textbook, la professoressa listed various Italian greetings on the whiteboard.

All the usual suspects were there:

Buongiorno

Buonasera

Arrivederci

After a few rounds of collective pronunciation, we were invited to take a break and gather in the kitchen for a cup of coffee, tea, or a glass of water, all the while addressing each other exclusively in English.

After all, it was only our first day.

No one engineered an escape during the break, and once we returned, la professoressa explained how we could all introduce ourselves and ask another person their name.

Once we had introduced ourselves to everyone else in the room, we sat down again to learn how we could point to others in the class and ask one of our neighboring students, 'What is his/her name?' and 'What are their names?'

Finally, we covered more casual and informal greetings, such as 'Ciao and Salve.'

Our first class was certainly great fun. It was very relaxed throughout, and everyone seemed very nice, especially and importantly, la professoressa.

In fact, if a fluent Italian speaker had asked me as I was leaving, 'Com'è andata oggi, Michele?'

I would have most certainly replied, 'Molto bene. Grazie.'

Chapter 3

Back for More

Once the machinations of the parking lot had been successfully negotiated, Emilia and I donned our name tags and made our way into the art room, to be greeted enthusiastically, in Italian, by those already there.

We responded in kind and joined in as others arrived.

It was an excellent way to set the tone for the day's endeavors, and everyone seemed to be looking forward to the class.

Textbooks were still on order for most of us, so la professoressa picked up from where we left off the previous week.

We covered introductions, both formal and informal, and gender-specific variations of the same. All of which amounted to a potential bear trap of embarrassment, if we should ever introduce a professional male colleague in an informal female context, for example.

As if that wasn't difficult enough, there were plural variations of the same and any number of likely responses.

The honeymoon was over, and I was already starting to struggle, just as la professoressa first uttered the phrase that I would find myself looking forward to each and every week.

"Prendiamo una pausa."

Several of us gathered in the kitchen, rinsing out glasses and cups, making coffee, and swapping notes, as I devoured the chocolate-coated muesli bar that was my cab fare to and from school.

I was relieved to learn that I wasn't alone when it came to struggling with formal and informal sentence structures. In fact, if anything, I was probably at the upper end of the knowledge spectrum, and I could demonstrate as much by explaining to a couple of others the various nuances of what we had just covered.

It was interesting to learn what other courses some of my classmates were taking at the same school. Kaye was studying French, as was Susanna, while Stefano was enrolled in a film appreciation class, and Barbara spent Thursday mornings playing Mahjong.

For the time being, however, Italian was more than enough for me.

We returned to class and were immediately, albeit very politely, 'told off' by la professoressa, for making too much noise in the kitchen and disturbing a lesson in the adjoining room. It was quite an odd circumstance, and something I daresay most of us hadn't endured for about fifty years.

Bronwyn then picked up from where we had left off, explaining that we could greet someone informally in Italian by asking, 'Come stai?'

A literal translation is something like, 'How is it that you are in a state of?' but it simply means, How are you?

Probable responses ranged from 'Bene' or 'Sto bene.' - I am well. to 'Benone' or 'Molto bene.' - Very well.

If anyone happened to be residing at the lower end of the wellness spectrum, they might reply, 'Sto male,' or sit on the fence and say, 'Così così.'

We were then instructed to complete another lap of the classroom, greeting each other once again, and asking what sort of state the other person was in.

If anyone was brave or bold enough to greet someone with the well-worn expression, 'Ciao Bella,' it certainly wasn't me, and it was probably just as well that I didn't already know the Italian for, 'I am really getting a bit sick of this, aren't you?'

Once we sat down again, we were introduced to the word, 'Andiamo,' a conjugation of the verb Andare, meaning, 'Let's go' or 'Shall we go?'

La professoressa explained that Italian people often ask questions by simply including an inquisitive inflection to the phrase they are uttering.

'Andiamo da Franco' could mean, 'Let's go to Franco's,' as much as 'Are we going to Franco's?' for example.

It was a single sentence that could have two slightly different meanings - simple enough.

To finish off, we learned a handful of new Italian words and phrases, including the word, 'compito.' It means homework, and this week's compito was to memorize a list of one hundred common Italian words ahead of a test next week.

Clearly, our third week was when the Pirellis would hit the road, and sort the uomini from the ragazzi.

Chapter 4

Last Man Standing

Three weeks in, and already the process of attrition had begun.

La professoressa took the roll, and two students hadn't shown up, hadn't sent an apology, and had almost certainly packed it in.

I couldn't be sure if it was the homework assignment or the prospect of a test, but the herd was already thinning.

Undeterred, Bronwyn pressed on, instructing us to close our books, place her list of one hundred common Italian words face down on the desk, and stand up.

She then enacted a rather cruel procedure, where she would select one student in turn, saying a single word in English.

The idea was for that student to respond with an accurate Italian translation (pronunciation included) or suffer the shame and indignity of being removed from the contest altogether.

Each of us was given a few seconds to respond, but anything more than that, and la professoressa told us to sit down.

Roberto needn't have bothered getting on his feet in the first place. To be fair, he was pretty low-hanging fruit. The first one picked, and the first one knocked out.

I nervously waited to be selected and happily avoided Roberto's fate, when I successfully recalled that the word always is 'sempre' in Italian.

Most of us did quite well, and it was the third round of questions before the pins started to fall.

I would often lament that I wasn't asked to translate a word that someone else was presented with, although to be fair, I did dodge a couple of bullets in the process.

By round six, just two of us were left, Emilia and me.

My friend had already demonstrated a tremendous capacity for learning languages, and it would be no shame to achieve an honorable second in a competition that had already laid waste to a pretty hot field.

All the same, I didn't particularly fancy the prospect of losing to her.

We traded verbal blows time and again with answers of 'tempo' and 'di nuovo,' before I was asked to translate the word 'out.'

I drew a complete blank. I was pretty sure the word featured toward the top of page three in 'La Professoressa's Hottest 100,' but it didn't come to mind, at least not in time anyway.

With the rest of the class perched on the edge of their seats, Bronwyn turned her attention to Emilia.

If she could correctly translate the word 'if' then I would be immediately and rather forlornly 'fuori' of the contest, with the honor, and spoils of victory showered upon my friend.

It would have been nice if she could have at least acted as though she had to think about it, racking her brain as she struggled to retrieve an answer from the deep, dark recesses of her mind.

Instead, without a moment's hesitation, or the slightest consideration for anyone else, she just blurted out "se," as if she had been doing this stuff all her life.

Show-off.

Chapter 5

Geography

O ur class convened in the art room for its fourth week, and by now it was abundantly clear that everyone intended to sit in the same place. It was as if we had all marked out our territory and no one should dare encroach upon another's patch.

I decided that in the future, I would time my arrival so that most, if not all, of the other students had already sat down, and before la professoressa herself entered the room.

This strategy would achieve two things:

1. I wouldn't suffer the indignity of being late.

2. I wouldn't have to call out "Buongiorno! Come stai?" a dozen times to greet every other student who entered the room.

Once la professoressa arrived, we were greeted as a collective for the first time with the phrase "Buongiorno tutti," before she wrote the words 'Come state?' on the whiteboard.

There are no prizes for guessing that the word 'state,' is a plural conjugation of the word 'stai' that we had learned the previous week, and an exercise in linguistic economy, whereby our teacher could now inquire of the entire class, in one fell swoop, just how it was that we were all currently in a state of?

We then discovered how to invite someone to 'come in.'

We would say 'Avanti,' and, to ask if we could introduce someone to them, 'Permesso le presento...'

For once, the name tags we were obliged to wear actually delivered a benefit.

In my case, constructing a clumsy and awkward introduction gave me just enough time to steal a glance at a classmate's tag in order to confirm their name.

If anyone's tag was facing the wrong way, it was simply a matter of asking them to turn it around, so I could confirm their last name, before reverting to a formal introduction.

I would then warmly thank that same person, using their first name all the while disguising the fact I had forgotten it in the first place.

Introducing a man formally as 'il signore' was simple enough, but whether or not a woman should be presented as 'la signora' or 'la signorina' was more problematic.

The honorific la signora is considered appropriate for married and older women. At the same time, la signorina is reserved for those considered younger and probably single. Marital status aside, exactly where the tipping point of age and maturity lay, no one could tell me.

Dopo la pausa, la professoressa presented us with a map of Italy that was printed on a dish towel, one that had been folded and left sitting in a drawer for some time, judging by the rectangular grid of creases that adorned the fabric.

She attached it to the whiteboard with a couple of large paper clips, before identifying some of the country's larger cities and more prominent regions.

As far as a basic introduction to Italian geography goes, it was crude but effective, and it allowed any number of students to identify parts of the country they had visited.

In Deborah's case, she regularly stayed in a small village called Introdacqua. It is located in the Abruzzo region, east of Rome, north of Naples, and 'just below that small red wine stain.'

La professoressa indicated where the city of Pisa is located, and after wrestling with a portable CD player for a few minutes, she played us an educational recording that presented a conversation between two people who were traveling throughout Italy.

Marco and Maria were visiting Pisa on vacation. They were sitting down to lunch at a restaurant in the city center and discussing in some detail what they intended to eat and drink.

They had a busy afternoon of sightseeing ahead of them, before making their way to the train station later in the day.

Both spoke fluent Italian, and I certainly warmed to Maria from the outset. I daresay she was a native, as her speech patterns and pronunciation were clear, warm, and articulate. Marco's were not. He was from Scotland (I suspect Glasgow) and suffocated his Italian with a sprawling, coarse, and entirely inappropriate accent.

The recording ruined the entire illusion, and I found myself completely ignoring whatever it was that Marco had to say. I couldn't care less what he had for lunch, or what he was looking forward to doing that afternoon, and I could only hope that he managed to miss 'il treno' later in the day so that Maria could present any subsequent installments of the recording alone.

The first part of our compito for the week was to list at least one place Marco and Maria planned to visit that afternoon and to write down two interesting things we could recall from their conversation.

I could think of one.

The remainder of il compito was to complete the quiz at the end of Chapter One in the textbook.

The quiz consisted of ten sections, with questions covering everything we had studied to date.

As if to reinforce the fact, a box featuring a giant question mark was printed directly above the first section of the quiz.

It was reposing to the left of a headline that read 'Still Struggling?'

The text in the box itself focused on the nuances of pronunciation, with advice regarding the various soft and hard sounds derived from the letters 'c, ci, ch, g, gh, and gli.'

For the time being, I wasn't getting too hung up on the nuances of pronunciation.

I was just happy the answers were printed in the back of the book.

Chapter 6

Nouns and Questions

Once la professoressa had taken the roll, it was clear that we had lost another student, Giuliana's husband Giovanni, no less.

He had confessed to his wife during the week that he was struggling to keep up and comprehend even the more straightforward elements of the language.

At which point, she suggested that he just wasn't trying hard enough.

Apparently, he didn't take it too well.

La professoressa then introduced us to nouns or 'sostantivi.'

Italian nouns are masculine or feminine, and should always be preceded by the appropriate male or female definite article.

For the most part, masculine nouns end in 'o' and feminine nouns end in 'a.' But there are several exceptions. Terrific.

The word for husband was top of mind for most of us at this stage. It is 'il marito' and, appropriately enough, masculine. In contrast, the word for wife is, needless to say, feminine and 'la moglie.'

A boy is 'un ragazzo' and a girl 'una ragazza.'

While the words for a man and a woman are 'un uomo' and 'una donna,' respectively.

At this point, I wanted to raise my hand and ask, "What was that Scottish uomo doing in that recording we listened to last week?"

But sadly, my Italian vocabulary didn't yet possess a sufficient range.

La professoressa then made good use of our immediate surroundings, explaining that the words for wall, roof, and floor were masculine, 'il muro, il tetto, and il pavimento.'

By contrast, the words for chair, whiteboard, and window were feminine, 'la sedia, la lavagna, and la finestra.'

I became well acquainted with la lavagna over the next few weeks and months, as armed with a cloth and a bottle of detergent, it was my job to clean it after each class.

Dopo la pausa, we were introduced to the concept of questions.

This meant that la professoressa could now sit back, relax, and revel in the spectacle of her students wandering around the room, pointing to various people and things while asking each other just who or what they were.

Given that a single conversation between any two students might consist of five or six questions, for Bronwyn it was the educational equivalent of an autopilot.

We were eventually spared the ordeal and sat down again before we were instructed to present something that we liked, or by literal translation from the Italian 'Mi piace,' to tell the class about something 'that is pleasing to me.'

The textbook showed a handful of examples, and those of us with dictionaries certainly had a rich source of material to call upon.

Not surprisingly, our next assignment was to write and read aloud three things that were pleasing to us.

I responded as follows:

Mi piace la caffè	Incorrect - il caffè.
Mi piace la vino rosso.	Incorrect - il vino rosso.

21

Mi piace la calcio.   Incorrect - <u>il</u> calcio.

Earlier in the day, la professoressa had told us that the appropriate male or female definite article should preface each noun.

Mathematically, I had a fair chance of getting at least one right, but I failed spectacularly.

Three attempts, all wrong.

Perhaps I should just stick to cleaning the whiteboard.

Chapter 7

Family

S oon after la professoressa had entered the room, and even before she had opened her binder to check the roll, she wrote the words 'la famiglia' - Family on the whiteboard. Thereafter, she defined some of the other members of our own families in Italian.

More importantly, however, she introduced us to a traditional Italian delicacy called 'il panettone,' a very light and tasty fruitcake that Italians often bake to celebrate Christmas.

What's more, she had brought one along that we all could share.

Once we had all indulged and polished off il panettone, she suggested we play a game of disappearing snowman.

She would draw a snowman on the whiteboard, and each of us would (in turn) stand up in front of the class, having composed a single word or a short phrase of Italian in our minds.

The other students were tasked with guessing or deducing each letter of the word or phrase in question, hopefully solving the puzzle before the various elements of the snowman (limbs, torso, and head) all melted away.

In the past, memory and pronunciation had been the key elements in any exercises we had undertaken, but in this case, it was spelling that came to the fore, with a number of us forced to make a shameful and embarrassing exit from our moment in the spotlight, having made an obvious and straightforward error.

I chose to play it fairly safe, sticking to single words with no more than three syllables, and as a result, all of my snowmen remained at least partially intact.

Even though we had spent no small amount of time eating cake during class, we were still invited to enjoy una pausa, and quietly make our way into the kitchen.

While we were all out of the room, la professoressa had placed some printed handouts on our tables.

The handouts presented a series of photographs, each showing a woman making a physical hand gesture, with an accompanying and explanatory portion of text printed underneath.

Once we returned, Bronwyn acted out some of the gestures herself and explained in what circumstances they might be considered appropriate and hopefully not too offensive, unless the intent was otherwise.

The first image showed a woman twisting the tip of an index finger into her cheek. This gesture indicated that a meal was 'delizioso' - delicious.

An appropriate facial expression that indicated boredom, disinterest, or outright frustration would accompany the second gesture.

It showed a woman holding both hands in the face of someone who was speaking to her. With her thumbs pressed against her fingers, she would move her hands back and forth as if to say, 'What on earth are you talking about?!'

To indicate that you think someone is crazy - 'pazzo/a,' simply point an extended index finger to the side of your head while staring at them in wide-eyed amazement.

La professoressa demonstrated the next gesture herself quite colorfully.

She extended her right hand and thrust it violently upwards, catching the crook of her elbow with her left hand, as she delivered an accompanying and forceful verbal instruction.

Emilia's friend Wendy was the only one who didn't understand exactly what it meant. There's always one. She appeared entirely bemused by the entire demonstration and asked Bronwyn rather naively, "What does that mean?"

Someone had to step up, and in this instance, it happened to be me.

"Think about it, Wendy," I said.

Other gestures followed that indicated stubbornness, the birth of an idea, and a somewhat threatening pose that suggested, 'If I catch you, I will kill you.'

This last one is communicated by staring at someone while biting the side of your hand.

My favorite gesture was enacted by looking at someone while raking your fingers outward and aggressively from underneath your chin. I daresay the gesture is clear enough for most people, but for those who are unsure, it communicates the phrase 'Me ne frego.' - I don't give a damn.

Slapping your forehead with the palm of your hand is an indication that you have forgotten something, and often accompanied by the expression 'Ho dimenticato,' while pressing one finger beneath an eye could indicate that the person you are speaking with is very clever, or it may be a warning for someone to watch out.

The last gesture on the list showed a woman extending the back of her hand forward while enacting a raking motion toward whomever she was speaking to.

It struck me as the sort of gesture that an angry teacher might use when insisting a mischievous student 'come here,' before they find themselves on the receiving end of a fierce verbal tirade.

I would be on the lookout for that one.

To finish the lesson, la professoressa introduced us to the concept of 'il malocchio' or the evil eye.

Il malocchio is an ancient Italian superstition, whereby someone might cast an envious, malevolent glare toward someone, or simply project such a feeling, and consequently bring about their misfortune or bad luck.

A bull's horn - 'un cornicello' is said to protect against the evil eye. Often worn as an amulet, and mistaken for a red chili, the cornicello charm is said to bring good luck to the wearer.

Another defense against il malocchio, is to make a horn-shaped gesture by pointing your hand downward, and extending your index and little finger while folding your thumb over your middle and ring fingers.

The Spanish prime minister formed that very same shape (behind his back) while walking alongside Italian prime minister, Silvio Berlusconi, before a meeting between the two leaders.

Can you blame him?

Chapter 8

Duolingo

One of my fellow students introduced me to a cell phone language-learning app called Duolingo.

It was a concept developed by a fellow who wanted to honor his mother (who was a school teacher), and it hosted any number of languages on its platform.

Needless to say, I wasted no time in signing up to learn Italian.

My Duolingo journey started with some fundamental words and phrases, and I gradually progressed through various modules, having completed five levels of increasing difficulty in each one.

Basics was followed by Phrases, Food, Animals, and Possessions.

One of Duolingo's helpful (if at times infuriating), features, is that completing an exercise, level, or module is only possible once all the correct answers to all of the questions have been entered.

It will forgive the odd minor spelling mistake, but for the most part, the rules stick fast.

Sometimes, I didn't understand or outright disagreed with a particular answer. In such a circumstance, I could select a graphic at the base of the screen that might offer an explanation.

More often than not, however, these explanations had been addressed previously, and posted by other members of the Duolingo community.

These people were invariably a pack of smart asses, and most of them would delight in demonstrating the fact they knew more about the language than me.

I gave some serious thought to deploying il malocchio a few times, but after realizing that any such tactic was very unlikely to succeed, I resorted to shouting a few choice words at the screen of my cell phone instead.

That didn't make the slightest difference either, and before long I decided that trying to argue the toss was more often than not a complete waste of time.

My Duolingo addiction continued to develop however, but only after I was reminded to complete the various elements of compito we had been set over the break, as the last thing I wanted to do was fall behind.

I finished the different written practice elements in the textbook and the quiz that concluded Chapter Two.

Confident that I now had greetings, simple questions, and a few basic nouns under control, I was looking forward to our next lesson.

Chapter 9

This and That

Next up, we were introduced to days of the week, or 'i giorni della settimana.'

The months of the year soon followed.

'Giorni e mesi,' - Days and months, further expanded our vocabulary, and importantly, no one could ever say about me again, 'He doesn't even know what day it is!'

La professoressa then introduced us to three important verbs:

Essere	to be
Avere	to have
Andare	to go

Each verb had its own conjugation structure, and we would need to remember each one if we hoped to progress with our studies and further develop our knowledge.

A few sample sentence structures using individual conjugations of these same three verbs were:

Sono confuso.	I am confused.
Ho mal di testa.	I have a headache.
Voglio andare a casa.	I want to go home.

This is just off the top of my head, you understand.

When it came to verb structures, I took a degree of comfort from the fact that some of the other students in the class seemed to be having even more trouble than me, but all the same, it was a challenging exercise to see a classmate struggling to answer a simple question or to translate a short sentence.

If there was a hierarchy of knowledge and ability in our class, then Roberto was firmly entrenched at its base. Why he even bothered showing up each week was a mystery to me. Each time la professoressa invited him to contribute, the rest of us had enough time to wander into the kitchen, make a cup of coffee, and return, before he eventually, and inevitably gave up.

What started as a painful experience to witness became something of a sideshow, as the rest of us would wait patiently in the sincere and forlorn hope that Roberto might actually provide a plausible, if not entirely correct, answer.

After checking and explaining the answers to the previous week's compito, la professoressa presented us with two common words that would prove essential building blocks in the structure of our Italian vocabulary.

Questo and quello mean 'this and that,' respectively. At least, they do when they precede a masculine noun, such as, 'libro,' for example.

If they precede a feminine noun, such as 'stanza' - the word for room, it means you have made a mistake.

In that instance, each word should transform to be 'questa or quella,' depending upon whether you are referring to this room or that room.

Just prior to la pausa, Bronwyn asked one of us, "Che giorno è?"

Anyone but Roberto could be expected to answer, 'Oggi è lunedì.'

She then asked me specifically, "Michele, che mese è?"

I seized the opportunity to demonstrate that I had been paying attention for the past few minutes and answered confidently, "Questo mese è ottobre."

It was a modest success, and la professoressa appeared suitably impressed.

Not only had I used the word questo correctly, but I had remembered that the word mese, despite its ending, was singular and masculine. Although to be fair, I probably fluked that bit.

In any case, I could now stroll into the kitchen, celebrate with a cup of coffee, and ask Stefano what movies his film appreciation class had been watching recently.

When we returned to class, we saw that la professoressa had written four new verbs across the top of the whiteboard, with a column of personal pronouns on its left-hand side.

We were then invited to complete the correct conjugations for each verb. All of which, might seem incidental and labored, but it was an important step toward achieving a significant milestone - the construction of a complete sentence.

We were introduced to numbers to finish the week, perhaps because la professoressa would be away for the next two weeks celebrating her fiftieth wedding anniversary.

I lost track of what she was saying at this point, as I pictured her walking down the aisle, aged about seven. Perhaps that's what a healthy, outdoor lifestyle will do for you, but in any case, I am pretty sure she said that she would be spending the next week or two traveling to and from Niagara Falls.

We then learned how to count to twenty, and from there to one hundred.

It certainly helped that numbers in Italian were structured similarly to those in English, 'uno' being one, and 'ventuno,' twenty-one, for example.

In la professoressa's absence, a woman named Annika de Bruin would be filling in.

Annika was a very experienced language teacher, who was in charge of an Advanced Italian Class at the same school, a class that la professoressa herself was a member of.

Chapter 10

She's All Business

W e filed into class the following week to see that Annika, our substitute teacher, was already there.

She had the same black binder, containing the student roll, open on her desk, and she greeted us all in Italian as we entered the room.

By 11:30 am, we had all sat down and were quietly chatting, when Annika picked up a small brass bell from her desk and began ringing it vigorously.

Everyone immediately stopped talking, and we all sat up straight while paying attention.

In my case, I found myself transported to my second-grade class at Balwyn North Elementary School. Not since Mrs Innes managed to strike such unbridled fear into a group of seven-year-old children had I felt so intimidated by a teacher.

In the past, Bronwyn had decided to leave the roll open on her desk. The idea was that each of us would enter the room, and tick a box next to our name to confirm our attendance. I would often mark other people's names off as well, to save them the trouble of making a trip all the way to the front of the room.

Not anymore, at least not for the next two weeks anyway.

Annika read the roll aloud, calling out each student's name, wherever feasible, in Italian.

At which point each of us would confirm our presence by responding 'Presente' or 'Sono qui.'

If we knew someone was already in the building but not yet in the room, we could respond by saying 'Arriva.'

If no one responded at all and was probably absent, Annika would inquire of us, "Non c'è?"

It was a question to which some of the braver souls among us could answer, 'No. Non c'è.'

Annika then invited us to introduce ourselves to her and to present another student in the class.

I chimed in first with "Mi chiamo Michele," before gesturing to my right and adding "e lui è Roberto."

It was always going to be a bloodbath, so why not just get it out of the way early?

Annika stepped in front of her desk and walked toward Roberto, saying "Bene."

If only she had stopped there.

Sadly, she pressed on, asking him, "E tu, di che nazionalità sei?"

Roberto's face was a blank canvas.

There wasn't the faintest hint of recognition in his eyes, and it was as if Annika had just asked him to explain the core principles of quantum physics in Latin.

Eventually, someone was kind enough to call out, "What nationality are you?"

At that moment, there was a glimpse of self-assurance, and his face fairly lit up.

"Ah," he said confidently, looking at the written notes he had taken the previous week.

His index finger ran back and forth across the page a couple of times before it stopped, and he proudly announced, "Sono americana."

The rest of us cringed and cowered, as we saw him caught in Annika's crosshairs.

She stalked him menacingly, then stepped forward, saying sternly, "So you've had the operation, have you?"

It was like watching a train wreck in slow motion.

Roberto shifted uncomfortably in his seat, clueless how to respond. At the same time, Annika continued to execute a ruthless pincer movement that had him trapped, surrounded, and desperately short of ammunition.

"Americano," I offered.

"What?" he said.

"Sono americano," I said, "because you're a man."

"Sono americano," he muttered.

Annika spent the next few seconds trying to correct his pronunciation, but the cause was lost from the outset, and I feared the entire exercise had left him shattered, broken, and empty.

I didn't think for a moment we would see Roberto next week.

In fact, I would be surprised if we saw him dopo la pausa.

Chapter 11

Colors and Clothing

Annika rang her bell again the following week as the clock on the wall ticked over to 11:30 am. Only this time (in anticipation of as much) most of us were already paying attention and ready to go.

More than once, I glanced to my right to confirm that it really was Roberto sitting there, occupying the same seat that he had made his own for the past ten weeks.

I thought the only reason he might show up today would be to lodge a formal complaint with the office, but there he was with his textbook, paper, and pen, ready to take notes.

If he did manage to make it through to the end of the year, he shouldn't be rewarded with a certificate so much as a medal.

Annika then introduced us to colors, or 'i colori.'

Soon after, we were able to associate those same colors with the articles of clothing that many of us were wearing.

Annika would hold up a garment and ask, "Di che colore è?"

The answer to which may well be, 'Quella camicia è bianca.' - That shirt is white.

Combining our knowledge of numbers and colors, we were able to construct a short sentence, explaining how much some of our clothes cost and asking the same of someone else.

They may not have been the most elaborate conversations of all time, but it was certainly fun to ask a question of someone and thereafter understand/provide an answer.

We then adopted Bronwyn's strategy of wandering around the room, asking each other what color various people's clothes were, and to whom those clothes belonged.

Once that exercise was completed, we returned to our seats.

Annika then tested our newfound knowledge by producing a pack of colored pencils and asking each of us in turn the color of 'la matita' she was holding in her hand.

I am happy to say that we all passed that test with 'i colori volanti.'

Chapter 12

How Old Are You?

Bronwyn returned to class after her vacation and immediately insisted on escorting us into a veritable minefield.

This week, we would learn how to ask one another, 'Quanti anni hai?'- How many years do you have? Or more simply - How old are you?

It was a question that could be no less awkward and impolite, given our class was primarily populated by women.

When it came time to roam the room again, I thought perhaps Graham, Stefano, and I should stick together.

Possible answers to the question could range from:

Ho sessanta anni.	I am sixty years old.
Non so.	I don't know.
Non ricordo.	I don't remember.

Of course, another possibility was:

Non sono affari tuoi.	None of your business.

If anyone should insist on pursuing the issue, we could always use one of the more elaborate and aggressive gestures la professoressa had so eloquently demonstrated a few weeks back.

Happily, we were spared another wandering inquiry process, as Bronwyn distributed a handful of color photocopies that she had made from the pages of a different textbook.

Each page presented a photographic record of a girl named Lucia and her trip to Italy.

The first photograph was taken in Milan.

It showed Lucia sitting beside an imposing statue of a lion and outside a grand-looking cathedral.

A caption above the photo read, 'Ciao, mi chiamo Lucia. Sono in Italia, ma non sono italiana. Sono una turista.'

Lucia was explaining that although she is in Italy, she is not Italian. She is a tourist, although rather conveniently, one with an Italian name.

She describes il Duomo di Milano as 'bello,' before moving on and introducing us to the 'panorama spettacolare di Portofino.'

In the third photo, we find her in Venice admiring 'una bella gondola.'

She even takes time out to greet the gondolier, 'Buongiorno, signore. Come stai?'

The gondolier is kind enough to reply, 'Non c'è male, grazie.'

Personally, I thought he could have done a bit more to embrace the romantic quality of his Venetian environment and come up with something a bit more colorful and elaborate than, 'Not bad, thanks,' but of course, I didn't write the copy.

Lucia then moves on to Florence and eventually, Rome, where standing outside the Coliseum, some idiot riding past on a Vespa greets her with the well-worn phrase, 'Ciao Bella!'

She replies, 'Attento al traffico stupido.'

Good for you, Lucia.

The next chapter of her adventure reveals that she is in Italy to study Italian.

And where better to do that than il Centro di Studi Italiani?

Lucia registers and introduces herself to Signora Pasotto, who sits behind the front desk. She then confirms that she is 'un'americana' and her name is Lucy Burns.

She enrolls in 'Livello cinque' - Level five, and soon after meets a Dutch student named Anna Maria, whom she initially mistakes for a teacher.

Both girls are pleased to learn they are enrolled in the same class, at which point Anna Maria confirms their teacher's last name is Bucchi.

Lucia then asks Anna Maria if 'il professore è alto e bello? - is tall and handsome?

Anna Maria confirms that il professore is indeed 'alto e molto bello,' before we discover that la professoressa Bucchi is in fact, a woman and consequently, 'alta e bella.'

As the story progresses, the two students build a solid friendship, notwithstanding the fact Anna Maria has clearly developed quite a sizeable crush on her teacher.

A series of questions followed the various photographs and captions, all of which we were expected to answer in Italian.

The questions included the name of the school, and the class level that both girls were enrolled in, the name of the female Dutch student, their teacher, and whether or not la professoressa Bucchi was tall or short.

It was all pretty basic stuff, but challenging enough to decipher and good fun to translate and comprehend.

Following a simple story like this was helpful, and perhaps for the first time, I felt as if I was actually getting somewhere.

Dopo la pausa, la professoressa introduced us to the various seasons and times of day.

We then discussed the Italian climate and a range of temperatures that traverse a country, surrounded by no less than five different seas, that is subject to some occasional and quite violent volcanic activity.

We also learned that countless local festivals are held throughout the year in Italy, with more significant outdoor events generally scheduled during the summer months.

Religious festivals celebrating Christmas and Easter are observed nationwide, while major cultural events such as 'il

Carnevale di Venezia' and 'il Palio di Siena' attract tourists from all over the world.

Not to be outdone, even the smallest towns and villages will stage annual festivals and events, celebrating their region's food, wine, or patron saint.

Chapter 13

Thinning the Herd

It was now week twelve of Italian for Beginners.

La professoressa had studied the roll and confirmed that class numbers had thinned further.

The gestures lesson had seen Wendy off, and try, as he may, it had finally all proven too much for Roberto.

I don't want to seem mean, but it wasn't the worst thing that could happen.

Most of us were making steady progress and having a lot of fun. Yet, much of our weekly two-hour allocation had been devoted to people who were, to paraphrase Giuliana, 'just not trying hard enough.'

Bronwyn then reinforced the casual and relaxed learning environment she had created by teaching us the phrase, 'Diamoci del tu.'

It's a phrase that essentially means - Let's be on a first-name basis and keep things informal and friendly.

Happily, our class was just that.

There may have been one or two students who were more advanced than others, but for the most part, we were all pretty much at the same level and able to move forward together.

We recognized and celebrated this fact during la pausa, as many of us continued to engage in some rudimentary Italian conversation, that, for the most part, related to cups of coffee, portions of sugar, and glasses of water.

It might have taken us twelve weeks and half a lesson, but we had finally arrived at a point in the course where we could mimic the environment of a restaurant or café and order something to eat and drink.

La professoressa explained that the word for restaurant is, 'il ristorante' and what we might know as a café was most likely 'un bar' in Italy.

I then learned two interesting things about the word 'trattoria.'

The first was how to pronounce it correctly, and the second was that 'una trattoria' is more of a family restaurant, as opposed to 'un ristorante' which is likely to be a more formal environment.

We were then given a brief insight into Italian coffee culture.

An Italian bar will generally offer customers an espresso they can drink while standing at the counter, together with other varieties of coffee they might consume at a table.

Sitting at a table will almost certainly define you as a tourist, and ordering a coffee with milk, such as a cappuccino, any time after 10:00 am definitely will.

In Italy, coffee with milk is very much frowned upon. Such drinks are considered breakfast fare only and are rarely consumed later in the day or after a meal. But of course, if you are sitting at a table, and, despite your hard-won language skills, have already been identified as a tourist, it's probably okay.

Under no circumstances, however, should anyone ever be so lazy as to order a latte. The word 'latte' means milk in Italian, and there are no prizes for guessing what a barista is likely to present you with if you ever do place such an order.

Any number of bar, trattoria, and ristorante owners have been on to this particular tourist quirk for generations, and they will delight in bringing customers a glass of milk whenever they 'order' one.

Good luck to them. I think it's hilarious.

Clothing and colors were complicated enough, but the atmosphere of a restaurant was something else again. The list of food and drink options was endless, and that was before we had even asked for 'un tavolo,' or something as simple as 'un bicchiere d'acqua.'

We still had to navigate 'il menu' and 'la lista del vino,' before deciding what food and wine we would order.

Having mulled over the various options, we revised multiple conjugations of the verb, 'prendere,' as Italians are more inclined to take food or drinks when ordering them in a restaurant rather than have them.

We all had some way to go, but at least we knew now that a glass was, 'un bicchiere,' a bottle, 'una bottiglia,' and when we next visited 'un ristorante italiano,' we could only hope that our 'cameriere' would be patient enough to indulge our clumsy Italian and not spit in 'la zuppa.'

La professoressa then suggested that we undertake a class excursion the following week.

We would not meet in the art room of the school but at D.O.C. a trendy and authentic Italian restaurant in Greenpoint.

Bronwyn would confirm the booking, asking the owners and staff to speak to us in Italian wherever feasible.

This excursion would be our first 'real world test' and an opportunity to torture a handful of native Italians who had traveled to the U.S. on student and short-term working visas.

Compito was to study the D.O.C. menu, copies of which la professoressa happened to have on hand, ahead of next Monday.

At least that might give some unsuspecting cameriere a fighting chance.

Chapter 14

Lunch at D.O.C.

D.O.C. described itself as a pizza, mozzarella bar, and delicatessen, and as far as we could tell, it was about as authentically Italian as it gets.

I arrived just before midday to find a diverse and successful enterprise in full swing. A counter and cash register were located just inside the front door, with a generously stocked delicatessen to the right.

The delicatessen presented shelves with more bottles of olive oil than I could possibly count, and several large glass display cabinets that housed a vast array of exotic and delicious provisions. To my left was the restaurant section, with a kitchen and wood-fired pizza oven at the rear, and rows of rectangular tables arranged in front and across the floor. Smaller tables were located outside (beneath awnings and umbrellas) on a timber deck that bordered a side street.

More than half the class was there when I arrived. Seven were sitting with their backs to me, and another three faced the front of the building alongside la professoressa herself.

It looked to me as if the more recent arrivals had decided to sit across the table rather than next to her, and not wanting to exaggerate the issue, I walked over, pulled out a chair, said "Buongiorno professoressa," and sat down to her left.

Deborah arrived soon after and sat next to me.

Once the usual pleasantries had been dispensed with, we enacted a general headcount to work out who (if anyone) was still missing.

No sooner had we identified the fact that Stefano was not yet among us, when I caught sight of him crossing the street through a large window to my right, which allowed me to announce, "Ecco Stefano!"

The word ecco, meaning, here is, was an expression we had learned a week or two before, and I was delighted that I was able to use at least one word of Italian in the correct context at what was effectively our first public outing.

D.O.C. had a policy of employing native Italians and fluent speakers of the language, and as la professoressa had promised, we were immersed in the nuances of an Italian dining experience from the outset.

The menus, together with a list of 'i speciali' (hand-written in chalk on a blackboard and leaning against the pizza oven) presented the names of various dishes in Italian, with detailed descriptions in English.

The menu included a highlighted section that was headed, 'Why D.O.C. Pizza?'

The D.O.C. pizza dough had been evolving since 1969 (almost as long as me) and one of its many unique characteristics was that it featured stone-ground flour. What's more, D.O.C. pizzas were made with San Marzano tomatoes, buffalo mozzarella and organic EV olive oil.

All of which didn't mean that much to me, but it did sound pretty impressive.

The process was 'enacted with a passion and experience passed down from a previous generation, one that adopted a slow approach and exercised a patient restraint.'

Notably, all those involved claimed to be artisans and, above all, proudly Italian.

I ordered a pizza, together with 'un bicchiere di vino rosso.'

I enjoyed both very much while swapping slices with Deborah's own pizza selection from i speciali.

The event proved to be a great success, as we could all enjoy ourselves and each other's company while revising our language skills without a textbook in sight.

Before long, the plates had been cleared away, and we were invited to submit our coffee orders.

When it came to my turn, I followed suit with one or two others and called out, "Latte, thanks."

A split second later, I was reaching forward and leaning down to nurse the sharp pain that was now throbbing in the bone of my right ankle. La professoressa had very soundly, and quite expertly, kicked me under the table, while berating me with the words, "Caffè latte!"

Not realizing that corporal punishment hadn't been outlawed at the LLI, I apologized for not adhering to the coffee culture lesson she had presented to us the previous week.

Il cameriere returned a few minutes later with all of our orders.

As he was standing on the other side of the table, holding my cup aloft, he inquired aloud, "Latte?!"

I reached over, said, "Grazie," and accepted my cup.

I put it down on the table in front of me, then turned to la professoressa (while pointing at said cameriere) asking her, "Are you going to tell him off as well?"

"Oh, he's been here too long," she said.

When it came time to settle the check, I was nominated to speak with one of the staff members on everyone's behalf and ask if we could all pay 'il conto' separately.

I watched a handful of D.O.C. employees scurrying back and forth across the restaurant floor as they ferried dishes to and from the kitchen, before I settled on my prey, like a starving lion stalking an unsuspecting antelope.

I mentally rehearsed my pitch a few times, and encouraged by my classmates, I stood up, walked over, and did my best to deliver the phrase, "Mi scusi, ma è possibile dividere il conto tra noi tutti?"

Or something like that anyway.

La cameriera sighed heavily and looked at me with a blend of emotions that appeared to be equal parts frustration and boredom.

"I think it might be better if we just spoke English," she said.

Chastened and humbled, I returned to my seat, where a couple of eager classmates asked me, "How did you go?"

"Disastro," I said.

That final and crushing rebuke aside, our lunch excursion proved a terrific idea and a great success. The food was delicious, and it was a welcome break from the classroom, even if my own command of the language had let me down a bit.

We eventually decided that everyone would give me enough cash to cover their orders and that I would settle everything with the cashier.

I announced our table number and explained the equation before we found ourselves oversubscribed by twenty-eight dollars.

I handed over all the money that I had and pointing downward in a somewhat exaggerated fashion, said to her, "Ventotto dollari nello Tip Jar."

I then thanked her and every other staff member I could find, before I fare welled la professoressa together with my classmates, and slowly limped to the car.

Chapter 15

Back to Class

We returned to class and thoroughly debriefed our recent gastronomic excursion, explaining what we had ordered, eaten, and drunk.
Some people also listed the purchases they had made afterward in the delicatessen.

Importantly, everyone enjoyed themselves, and there was much laughter in the room as we discussed the various elements of the language that we had at least tried to deploy throughout.

Having no desire to spoil the mood, I made no mention of the infamous 'latte episode,' and the subsequent assault on my right ankle.

After confirming the day and date, la professoressa introduced us to the concept of 'Verbi regolari' - Regular verbs, together with the various endings that were associated with their individual conjugations.

She then decided to ask one of us what we were wearing that day.

That same person would then continue the sequence, asking a similar question, of another student, and so on.

I daresay she saw me sifting through the notes I had taken in an earlier lesson (one that had defined various items of clothing) as she asked me, "Michele, cosa porti oggi?"

Happily, I understood the question, and secure in the knowledge that I was wearing a navy blue jacket, I replied confidently, "Oggi, porto una giacca blu."

"Perfetto!" she responded, before inviting me to continue the sequence and ask the same question of a classmate.

I then turned and looked toward Graham, asking him, "Graham, cosa porti oggi?"

Graham confirmed that he was wearing 'un maglione verde' before the exercise continued around the room, with shoes, socks, and trousers, together with their respective colori, all being defined.

As if that wasn't enough, we were then introduced to the concept of, 'Verbi irregolari' - Irregular verbs.

Foremost among these was our old friend - Essere.

Essere was a crucial verb that would feature prominently in any number of grammatical structures down the track.

Another significant verb and Essere's partner in crime, as much as its importance to the language is concerned was - Avere.

We had learned previously that to ask a question in Italian, often one simply needs to add a curious inflection to what would otherwise be a simple statement of fact.

For example, I could ask someone, 'Do you have a book?' by saying, 'Hai un libro?'

To which that person might reply, 'Si, ho un libro.'

If their answer happened to be negative, it was simply a matter of placing the word 'non' at the start of the sentence - 'Non ho un libro,' for example.

Needless to say, we were soon all on our feet and wandering around the room, asking each other if we had a book, a jacket, a sweater, or pink trousers.

For the record, no one in the class had pink trousers. That was simply an opportunity for someone to present a negative answer.

Compito for the week was for us all to pair off, and compose what la professoressa described as, 'una commedia.'

The idea was to compose a short play consisting of a conversation between two people, confirming what day, date, and time they would do something. They could arrange to meet for coffee, go shopping, or revise their Italian homework, for example.

We had to develop our creations in the next few days and present them to the class the following week.

Conveniently at this stage, our class numbered ten students, and even though I sat next to Susanna each week, she had already teamed up with Deborah, who sat to her left.

Emilia's friend Wendy had bailed out of the class a few weeks back, so she and I decided to work together.

As the class drew to a close, and before I got up to clean the whiteboard, I sat quietly in my seat for a moment, wondering if one day I may impress someone to the extent they might say to me, 'Michele, tu parli l'italiano molto bene.' - Michael, you speak Italian very well.

Forse un giorno.

Chapter 16

La Commedia

I t wasn't Puccini by any stretch or anything Giuseppe Verdi needed to worry about, but Emilia and I did manage to perform a relatively competent commedia.

I emailed her a fundamental story outline the day after class, and we met at her apartment later in the week to develop and finalize our composition.

Our commedia presented the two of us engaged in a telephone conversation, during which we discussed how best to develop our commedia.

It was a kind of circular logic.

I 'called' Emilia on the phone, and after we had extended the usual greetings and polite inquiries of 'Buongiorno' and 'Come stai?' we were able to confirm that we were both 'Bene.'

We then stumbled over a few phrases related to telling time and that our class was held 'ogni lunedi,' before we finished by congratulating each other on a job well done.

I don't imagine for a moment that our performance ranked terribly high on the entertainment scale, but it did demonstrate the fact that we had been paying attention in recent weeks, and I for one reckon that should count for something.

No one's performance enlisted a standing ovation, as other students presented themselves, meeting for coffee, arranging to meet for coffee, and bumping into one another while shopping.

Dopo la pausa, we were given another colored photocopy handout titled, Capitolo Due.

It was a continuation of Lucia's Italian journey, and it introduced us to Carlo, another student at il Centro di Studi Italiani.

In the first sequence of photos, Carlo explains that his father had insisted he travel to Italy during his summer school vacation to improve his language skills.

Carlo thinks this is very unfair and a complete waste of time, as, in his opinion, he already speaks Italian very well.

We had a few minutes to scan the images and to read the text on the first page before we had to confirm how old Carlo was, his nationality, what subjects he was studying, and the opinion that Anna Maria, in particular, had formed of him.

For the record, Carlo is nineteen years old, he is English with an Italian father, studying Italian, ceramics, and music, and importantly, Anna Maria thinks he is 'not shy.'

I took 'not shy' to mean, rather full of himself.

We discovered that the students gathered at 'il bar centrale nella piazza' whenever they had time, and that, in Carlo's opinion, all the other students worked too hard.

In return, Lucia and Anna Maria don't bother to speak much with Carlo, as in their opinion, he is both 'noioso e pigro' - boring and lazy.

Tough break, Carlo.

As the story progresses, we discover that Carlo thinks Lucia has 'un sorriso carino' - a lovely smile. However, his romantic ambitions suffer a crippling setback when he fails to bring a pen or textbook to class.

Suffice it to say, Lucia is not impressed.

We do discover, however, that Carlo has one very significant and redeeming characteristic. His grandmother lives nearby, and she offers to cook Carlo and his friends a meal.

Carlo decides that in order to win Lucia's heart, he will invite all his classmates to dinner, and prepare his own 'Minestrone Speciale' that same evening.

The tactic proves a great success, as we see Lucia, Anna Maria, and another student named Caterina, all seated 'alla tavola della nonna di Carlo.'

They are all eagerly holding out their empty plates so that Carlo can replenish them with a second serving of his signature soup.

Caterina tells Carlo, 'Sei un tesoro' - You are a treasure. Anna Maria says, 'Sei molto bravo, Carlo,' and Lucia assures Carlo he is very nice and that he too has 'un sorriso carino.'

It must have been one hell of a soup.

La professoressa then worked her way around the room, asking each of us, in turn, a question that related to the story.

Others were asked, 'How old is Carlo?' and 'What nationality is Carlo?' together with where he was studying and what subjects he was taking.

When it came to my turn, she asked, if, in my opinion, Carlo and Lucia were friends.

I answered, "Prima o dopo la zuppa?" - Before or after the soup?

Chapter 17

A Practical Application

Emilia was obliged to attend a medical appointment in Tribeca one day.

She didn't fancy battling the peak hour traffic or finding a space to park her car, so I offered to drive, drop her off, and then collect her on the way home, 'dopo un caffè.'

A brief coffee excursion would allow me to immerse myself in the heart of Little Italy and enjoy 'un caffè' in one of the many 'bar e ristoranti tradizionali' that populate the district.

I practiced ordering a coffee in Italian several times en route.

I even managed to compose as much aloud to myself (while executing a reverse parallel park) before I confidently strolled into what appeared to be an authentic and traditional Italian establishment.

The café itself was large but quiet. It was modestly lit, with small, dark wooden tables dotted throughout and long timber bench seats set against the walls.

A handful of patrons were already seated inside, all older men, sitting alone.

Each appeared to be nursing an espresso, while one had his head buried in an Italian language newspaper.

For all I knew, I could have been magically transported to Naples or Milan.

I could see a large coffee machine, next to which stood a very tall, dark, and impossibly handsome fellow. He looked quintessentially Italian and wore a white linen shirt with a short, black apron tied around his waist.

He was polishing several glasses with a crisp, white cloth, and as I approached, he stopped what he was doing, casually put both hands on the surface of the counter, looked me squarely in the eye, and said, "Ciao."

In that instant, I completely forgot the script I had rehearsed several times just minutes before.

I had managed to multi-task quite effectively up to this point, and recite the words, "Vorrei un caffè con latte caldo per favore," while parking the car, but when presented with the opportunity to actually execute the phrase, I completely froze and eventually mumbled a clumsy and pathetic, "Hello."

I really should have quietly left at that point and returned when I could actually present a simple sentence in the language I had been learning for the past six months.

Instead, I broke with convention, as it was after 10:00 am, and ordered a caffè latte entirely in English.

I then sat slumped on one of the bench seats near the door, feeling disappointed and embarrassed.

Perhaps the crushing communication rebuke I experienced at D.O.C. had eroded my confidence more than I realized.

The café was a quaint and quiet environment to sit and relax, all the same.

There was no music playing, no televisions mounted to the wall, and the venue's ambience was friendly and warm.

I vowed to return one day and give the whole process of ordering a coffee another try.

A few days later, we returned to class and revised the written practice exercises that had been set as the previous week's compito.

The first of these exercises focused on correctly using the verb, 'essere' when confirming someone's nationality.

In my case - 'io sono australiano.'

La professoressa then went to great pains to illustrate that to pronounce the letters, 'au' correctly in Italian, one needs to make an 'ow' sound.

Rather like someone has just kicked you in the ankle, under the table at a restaurant, for example.

Next up, we answered a series of questions in the textbook that inquired about the status of Mario's car, his sofa, trousers, suitcase, male friends, female friends, and shirt.

Just as we were coming to terms with the fact that Italian adjectives must agree with the gender and number of the noun they are modifying, we were presented with a series of exceptions, adjectives that were invariable and did not change, regardless of gender or plurality.

If I could master this, then all things considered, ordering a coffee should be a walk in the park.

Chapter 18

Pronunciation

We kicked things off the following week by re-visiting the concept of pronunciation.

La professoressa supplied us with a handout that presented a short section on vowels, a much longer element devoted to consonants, and the sounds that specific letters should make when they appear in isolation or the company of others.

I also discovered the accents that appeared when written or printed above vowels at the end of words were actually there for a reason.

They weren't there as some subtle embellishment or decoration after all, but to demonstrate that the vowel in question should be exaggerated and emphasized when the word is pronounced.

As complicated as it may sound, it all made perfect sense.

Words simply 'sounded right' when pronounced correctly, and when sufficient emphasis was placed on certain vowels, or a word's first syllable.

I thought it was good fun to embellish my own pronunciation, and I had (apparently) developed a habit of using rather colorful hand gestures as I did, much to the amusement of my classmates.

It wasn't something I was consciously aware of, and whether or not it actually helped, I really can't say, but most of the others seemed to think it was pretty funny.

Class numbers would be further reduced for the next few weeks as Deborah was embarking on her annual sojourn to the village of Introdacqua in the Abruzzo region of Italy.

She told us all about the village and some of the unique characteristics of Abruzzo, which prompted others to discuss some of their own Italian vacations.

I delighted in recalling the ten days a group of friends and I spent living in a Tuscan villa (just outside Siena) while making road trips to Florence, Pisa, and Rome in a rental car.

The only downside for me was that every city we visited was littered with tourists, but given I was one of them and therefore part of the problem, I really had no right to complain.

Graham then shared a wonderful anecdote of when he found himself at a train station, standing at a ticket window with an Italian phrasebook. He was trying to secure some return tickets to his desired destination, and as he did so, the woman in the office enthusiastically encouraged his every word. She would smile and gesture warmly as she coaxed each awkward syllable from his lips, like a proud parent reaching toward an excited toddler taking its first few steps.

Once he had finished, he closed his phrasebook and looked up, just as the woman on the other side of the window shouted, "Bravo!"

She applauded him generously, clapping her hands together as if he had just scored the winning goal for Italy in the dying seconds of the World Cup Final.

God forbid people like that are ever replaced by machines.

Dopo la pausa, we completed the quiz at the end of Chapter Five, which proved to be a tribute to the long-since departed Roberto, as we practiced pronouncing different nationalities. Be they male, female, or plural.

La professoressa then battled with the portable CD player again, as we passed copies of a photocopied script to one another.

Her 'Starting the Day' handout presented some dialogue between Beppe and Marisa - two people who had just gotten out of bed.

We listened to the recording of their conversation as they greeted one another, enquiring as to how well the other had slept, and whether or not Marisa would like a cup of coffee.

The couple then confirmed the date, while discussing the fact they had tickets for an exhibition that same day.

A series of questions followed, most of which were presented in a 'vero o falso' - true or false format.

This was a shame, as such a format would have given Roberto a rough chance of getting a few right.

The next chapter in the textbook was titled - Learning the Present Indicative.

This chapter presented something of a challenge for me, as I wasn't entirely sure what that meant in English, let alone Italian.

Happily, the first section covered much of what we had already learned, outlining a conjugation of the verb Parlare as an example.

We then enacted a process whereby we all asked each other if we spoke Italian before completing a series of questions that confirmed whether or not various others in the class spoke Italian, English, French, or curiously Russian.

Soon after, my verbal and written practice was awash with present indicative questions as to how often I, or a classmate, bothered to practice our Italian rather than watching television.

Chapter 19

Food and Drink

The following week, we revisited the verb Mangiare - to eat. Before being introduced to a couple of other verbs, namely:

Bere — to drink

Dare — to give

We then spent the next few minutes asking each other what we wanted to drink, what we were drinking, and to whom we intended to give a specific drink to.

The written practice that followed defined an array of drink-related activities, before we focused on a general 'what and where' of people's eating and drinking habits.

It was hard work, and I found myself craving something more robust than a coffee by the time we had finished.

Dopo la pausa, la professoressa asked each of us in turn what we usually had for breakfast - 'la colazione.'

Happily, she had written a helpful reference list on the whiteboard during the break. It listed the Italian words for coffee, tea, orange juice, cereal, yogurt, toast, sausages, and eggs.

That meant all we really needed to do was remember the words for breakfast, eat, and drink.

When it came to my turn, I answered, "Per la colazione, io mangio le uova con pane tostato e bevo caffè." - For breakfast, I eat eggs with toast and drink coffee.

I scored a bonus point when it came to the eggs, as I had correctly used the plural preposition 'le' with the correct if typically single feminine form of the noun in 'uova.'

Italian eggs are non binary, and they also disobey standard rules of mathematics. In Italian, a single egg is 'un uovo' (masculine), but a plural number of eggs is 'le uova' (feminine).

Don't ask me why. Perhaps it came down to a simple proofreading error after some ancient Roman scholar made a mistake while drafting a Latin dictionary.

Next up, we were presented with a script featuring a conversation between Tom and Kate, a couple who were renting a house in Portofino for a week.

It was titled - 'Andiamo a fare la spesa.' - Let's go shopping.

The original script was in Italian and accompanied by an English translation that appeared to have been drafted by the same people who write the assembly instructions for flat-pack furniture manufactured in Taiwan.

Most of us did a good job with the Italian. At the same time, the accompanying English translation continued to demonstrate how not to do it.

In short, Kate wanted to catch a bus into the town center and go shopping.

In contrast, Tom wanted to stay in the house and watch whatever sport was on TV - as you do when you have just traveled thousands of miles to visit an exotic foreign destination.

Kate listed several objectives, which included visiting the post office, delicatessen, and dry cleaners.

Tom countered with the various times that tennis, golf, and soccer were on TV.

Eventually, Kate travels into town alone, and she returns a few hours later with 'molto cibo' - a lot of food, 'una nuova valigia' - a new suitcase, and 'delle scarpe costose' - some expensive shoes.

I hope she used her husband's credit card.

Tom then complains that his 'moglie' - wife, 'è pazza' - is crazy.

The script didn't actually confirm that Kate's husband 'è un limone assoluto' - is an absolute lemon.

Still, it's not as if we couldn't figure that much out for ourselves.

Compito was to read a short handout titled, 'Alla Trattoria,' to study its accompanying vocabulary and answer a handful of questions that followed the text.

Alla Trattoria confirmed that it is possible to eat very well and relatively inexpensively in just about every Italian city, and that some trattorie will offer customers a fixed-price menu.

The questions that followed were all in Italian, and notwithstanding my answers were a bit clumsy and awkward, the fact that I could understand the questions in the first place was certainly encouraging.

Chapter 20

Same Time Next Year

I f there is a prize for the language with the most variations
corresponding to the English definite article 'the,' then my
money is on Italian.

It can boast seven, and it's probably just as well we weren't
presented with all of them on our first day of school. Otherwise,
mine may have been the briefest educational journey of all time.

In what was our final class for the year, we took a short test
where we had to place the correct form of the definite article
before any number of nouns that defined numbers of men,
women, colors, clothes, animals, food, and nationalities before a
heavy downpour of rain heralded an introduction to 'il tempo' - the
weather.

Suffice it to say, the first words we learned were 'il tempo fa
brutto,' - the weather is awful, unless of course, you were
'un'anatra' - a duck, in which case, il tempo was probably bello.

One of the challenges we continued to face when listening to
people speak Italian was how quickly they did so, and the fact that
syllables, words, and entire sentences seemed to run together
without the speaker ever drawing breath.

I had long argued that minor grammatical errors in
conversation were of little significance, given everyone speaks so

quickly, that no one has the slightest chance of picking up the occasional mistake anyway.

Of course, it was never possible to ask a newsreader, television or film actor, 'Can you speak more slowly, please?'

However, we were introduced to the concept of News in Slow Italian, a website and cell phone app that does exactly what it says it does. It delivers up-to-date news bulletins in Italian at about half the pace that one might typically expect.

It was still difficult to comprehend exactly what people were saying, but I was able to detect the odd word and pick up the general thread of each particular bulletin all the same.

I decided that News in Slow Italian and Duolingo would keep me up to the mark during the holidays, as la professoressa delivered some terrific news.

She had decided to continue with our Beginners Class into its second year and to present a class that the school would define as Italian Two.

This meant we would have the same teacher, working through the same textbook, with most of the same students going into our second year.

Apart from a two-month break over the summer, the transition would be relatively seamless.

It was great news, as our group had formed a good rapport over the course of the year, and we had all become very fond of la professoressa.

Discussion then turned to how we should mark and celebrate the end of our first year.

We had all gathered for lunch at D.O.C. a few months before, but for our end-of-year breakup, we decided to book a table at a smaller restaurant called 'Onde' for lunch.

Onde was well known to some of my classmates and operated by a gregarious Italian fellow they knew as Gerry.

I was nominated to make a phone call during class, and we booked a table for 10 the following week.

Dopo la pausa, Deborah managed to enhance the celebrations when, having just returned from Italy herself, she presented each of us with a small parcel of 'confetti' that she had bought in Sulmona and brought home with her.

Confetti is a traditional Italian delicacy that is associated with significant family events, such as weddings and baptisms.

Each morsel consists of an almond, encased in a colorful and crisp sugary coating.

Thought to date back to Roman times, confetti is often presented in small pouches (as a gift) and always in an odd number, as an even quantity is considered bad luck.

The English word confetti is clearly derived from the same, but Italian confetti should never be confused with the tiny portions of colored paper that people in Western nations make a habit of throwing at weddings.

Aside from the fact that doing so is likely to cause an injury, traditional Italian confetti is far too delicious to throw at anyone.

Ahead of the summer holidays, we were presented with two colorful handouts that might prove helpful over the next couple of months.

One was titled, 'Vacanze' - Holidays and the other, Sport.

Each depicted several people engaged in the sort of activities that many of us might find ourselves doing while on vacation. There were illustrations of people 'praticare lo sci nautico' and 'giocare al calcio,' but I reckon waterskiing and playing soccer were probably beyond most of us by this stage.

Finally, we were presented with a reference sheet listing any number of different foods and drinks, together with some helpful restaurant vocabulary that we might recognize if anyone was brave enough to speak to us in Italian next week, and ask what we would like to order.

La professoressa had also drafted a typical restaurant conversation on a single sheet of paper.

It concluded with someone ordering, 'Un caffè latte, per favore.'

I couldn't help but think that last entry was there for my benefit in particular.

Studying the document would give us all a fighting chance next week, and provide us with a viable launching pad ahead of our second year.

As everything wound up for the day, and before we all wandered into the parking lot, we were reminded to meet one another at Onde next Monday 'per il pranzo,' and our final class for the year.

Chapter 21

Onde

As we gathered at Onde, I noticed that la professoressa was wearing a pair of rather sporty new spectacles, and I seized the opportunity to earn a few points ahead of next year by telling her how much I liked them.

"Mi piace il tuo occhiali, Bronwyn," I said, anticipating a kind smile and a response such as, 'Grazie, Michele.'

Instead, she repeated my compliment in its correct plural form, "Mi piacciono i tuoi occhiali."

She was nothing if not professional.

Onde was a small and cozy trattoria that backed onto a parking lot. To this day, I am not sure if it has any presence on the street.

The restaurant was housed in a converted garage, and we were all seated at a long rectangular table set to its right-hand side.

The owner greeted some of my classmates like long-lost friends, and all of us with an infectious enthusiasm and generous warmth that left many of us with the impression he really was delighted to see us.

I am not sure if anyone had 'worded him up' beforehand, or if he made a habit of greeting all of his customers this way, but he marched toward our table with his arms stretched wide and won us all over with an excited and gracious, "Buongiorno! Come stai!"

Once we had all sat down, it was clear that most of us had made it on time. I sat at the head of the table with Bronwyn a few feet to my right. Barbara was sitting between us, and I was counting on her to act as a human shield should I stuff up my coffee order again.

As we greeted one another and presented our drink orders to la cameriera, we took a moment to remember the fallen. Those students who had enrolled and showed up to our first class, but who hadn't managed to stick it out for the entire year.

Susanna wasn't there as she had moved interstate, and we had lost Stefano a couple of months back, without any explanation or reply to several emails.

Giovanni had bailed out early when his wife told him he 'just wasn't trying hard enough,' and the gestures session had seen Emilia's friend Wendy off.

Our most significant casualty was, of course, Roberto.

For several weeks, the man had struggled and fought with all of the courage and dignity he could muster. Roberto, the man who had clung so bravely to his unlikely Italian dream, before I served him up on a platter, and Annika went through him like a speeding locomotive bursting through a crepe paper banner.

We were just about the only people at Onde that day, and while the menu was limited, the setting was quintessentially Italian, and I daresay we all found a pasta or pizza dish that managed to fit the bill.

The food was delicious, and the wine was wonderful before someone invited Gerry to tell us about the gastronomic tours of Italy that he marketed and hosted.

Each tour had a regional focus, and each one, as far as I could tell, was insanely expensive.

I assumed that his quoted price included airfares, accommodation, food, and wine.

In fact, none of those things were included, and I was left thinking, "Why on earth would you battle away operating a restaurant like this if you can find enough people who are both wealthy and gullible enough, to pay you thousands of dollars a day to drive them around Italy visiting a few restaurants and wineries?"

He was a lovely man, and I am sure he would be a very gracious and entertaining guide, but I would be surprised if people were queuing around the block to sign up for one of his tours.

Once our meals had been devoured and the coffee had arrived, it was time for us to make a presentation to la professoressa.

We had passed the hat around a couple of weeks before and cobbled together enough cash to present her with a big bunch of flowers, and a limited edition print of one of Emilia's paintings, with both gifts going over tremendously well.

It fell to me to make a speech, and on everyone's behalf, I told Bronwyn how much we had enjoyed ourselves and how grateful we all were for her patience and generosity.

It was easy to forget that la professoressa acted as a volunteer and that she received no financial reward or return for all of the time she devoted, both during classes and in their preparation. The modest tuition fees we had all paid at the start of the year were designed to cover the cost of printing a few name tags, keeping the lights on in the office, and the photocopier in reasonable working order, nothing more.

We could all count ourselves tremendously lucky to have stumbled upon an opportunity presented to us by someone as kind, generous, and devoted as Bronwyn Street.

And perhaps best of all, we could look forward to doing it again next year.

Chapter 22

Italian Two

Our Beginners Class had progressed into its second year. In the process, it had been re-defined as Italian Two and re-opened for enrollment, allowing anyone with at least one year's experience studying Italian to join.

We had been allocated a different room, just beyond the kitchen and a little to the right of the art room.

The new room was rectangular, and it didn't have a six-inch-wide timber pole standing in the middle of it. As a consequence, it presented a more practical classroom environment.

A previous class had been kind enough to arrange several folding tables to reflect the room's shape. There was enough space for four people to sit across the top end and eight along each side, before anyone needed to encroach upon what was clearly la professoressa's section, given its proximity to the TV monitor, and whiteboard.

When I arrived, a handful of new students were already seated on the far side of the room, and one new one was sitting opposite them closer to the door.

I collected one of the more sturdy chairs on offer, placed it next to hers, and sat down.

I soon learned that her name was Linda and that she had studied Italian some years before when she spent a couple of years living in Florence.

All nine surviving beginners filed in eventually, and by the time la professoressa arrived, and confirmed the roll, it was clear that our number had swelled to eighteen.

Bronwyn then asked that we each introduce ourselves and explain how long we had studied Italian.

We soon learned that the enrollment criteria listed on the school's website of 'at least one year's experience learning Italian,' had been well and truly covered by most.

Some had in fact chalked up several years, with one woman explaining that she had studied the language (albeit several years before) at college with la professoressa herself.

We weren't twenty minutes into our second year, and already the beginners had fallen behind.

La professoressa introduced the new students to the textbook before asking us all to secure a copy of Short Stories in Italian.

This small paperback book featured an illustration of a smartly dressed couple riding a Vespa on the cover, with the Coliseum in the background.

As per the textbook, in Italy, it would appear that wearing sunglasses is considered a far more critical safety consideration than a helmet when riding a Vespa.

La professoressa then presented us with a detailed breakdown of the elements we would cover each week and over the course of the year, together with a listing of who would be in charge of each class.

Bronwyn explained that she had been awarded a two-week scholarship to a language school in the city of Macerata, in the Marche region of Italy.

The school offered training courses to Italian students and for teachers who taught the language in foreign lands.

Bronwyn would take charge of our class for its first four weeks before handing the reins, once again, to Annika for two.

According to the course outline, our objectives for the year were as follows: 'To cover basic speaking, reading, writing, and listening skills, focusing on applied language, to deal with others in everyday settings and situations relevant to travelers in Italy, or those interacting with Italian people.'

In other words, 'Develop the capacity to order a coffee in an Italian café without making a complete fool of yourself.'

Name tags proved handy at the break, as most of us gathered in the kitchen and introduced ourselves to the new students.

We returned to class a few minutes later, to find that we each had a photocopied short story placed on the table in front of us.

The purpose of this first exercise was for la professoressa to be either reminded, or to get some idea, of our various pronunciation skills, and she asked that we each read a paragraph or two aloud.

The story was written by a teenage girl named Sofia. She was going on vacation to Italy with her parents and younger brother. As we joined them, Sofia, her brother, and her parents had packed their bags and were making their way to the airport.

By the time the story reached me, Sofia was in the process of describing herself physically. She explains that she has 'occhi marroni' - brown eyes, 'capelli castani' - brown hair, and 'gambe lunghe' - long legs.

I saw Bronwyn sitting comfortably at the front of the class and quietly drifting along as we read the story, so I decided to pull the proverbial rug out from under her.

Sofia went on to say 'e ho una bocca grande.'

"That means she has got a fat ass," I said.

It took a second or two for la professoressa to respond.

She stared at her copy of the script for a moment, then looked at me and snapped, "It does not say that! It means she has got a big mouth! You know it means she has got a big mouth!"

"Oh. Yes, of course it does," I said.

I apologized, blaming the fact I had been away recently and that my translation skills were a little rusty as a consequence.

She didn't believe a word of it.

In any case, our compito was to write a few lines explaining what we had each done during the holidays.

Our compositions should take the form of a letter, starting with

Cara Bronwyn

Durante le vacanze...

and concluding with,

Tanti saluti

Michele

After consulting a dictionary and doing a bit of grammar research, I was able to write, "Ho lavorato sul mio nuovo libro. Penso che sia molto buono." - I worked on my new book. I think it's pretty good.

Chapter 23

The New Normal

The most significant development to emerge during the break was the fact that every Monday morning there was a custom-built coffee truck standing at the edge of the school parking lot, complete with an espresso machine, refrigerator, take-out cups in two sizes, and more often than not, a short queue.

The venture was the brainchild of a local girl named Amy, who had built her mobile coffee enterprise on the back of a medium-sized cab chassis vehicle and an infectious enthusiasm.

She had secured permission from the school to turn up each week, and she continued to do a brisk trade from the Italian Two class in particular.

Amy's van was the first order of business for many of us, and given Graham, Linda, and I were unfailing regulars, we would often submit coffee orders in addition to our own when we saw each other drive into the parking lot.

Showing up to class without a coffee in hand soon became as unrealistic and foolish as showing up without a textbook, and sipping one during the first few minutes of each lesson was indeed the new normal.

Week one of Italian Two had failed to see anyone off, and a full complement of students filed into class the following Monday.

Some of us were still without textbooks, and most were still waiting for the short stories, so la professoressa raised the bar, writing the following question on the whiteboard:

Cosa farai oggi dopo la classe?

What are you doing today after class?

In the first instance, we were expected to translate the question, without revealing as much to anyone else, and secondly to answer it aloud and in turn.

Some of our more experienced students seized the opportunity to demonstrate that they really should have enrolled in an intermediate, if not advanced Italian class, by constructing and presenting answers that expressed the fact that they were going to the hairdresser, meeting friends for coffee, or taking the dog for a walk, provided it wasn't raining.

By contrast, I offered, "Vado a casa."

I am the first to admit that mine wasn't a particularly challenging answer, but I really was just going home after class, to say nothing of the fact I didn't need a haircut and I don't own a dog.

La professoressa then listed several questions on the whiteboard, explaining how we could ask what people were saying, what they wanted to say, and how to ask what various words and phrases actually meant.

She then very kindly, concluded her presentation by teaching us how to say, 'Non capisco' - I don't understand.

Dopo la pausa, we made our first tentative foray into the past tense, as we were told how to say or write, 'I went for a walk.'

In Italian, a walk is 'una passeggiata,' which has always struck me as a very elaborate term for such a basic activity. What's more, the simple expression, 'I went for a walk,' could utilize no less than three of the verbs we had already studied. Namely, Essere, Andare, and Fare, and conjugations of all of them appeared in the sentences, 'Sono andato per una passeggiata' or 'Ho fatto una passeggiata.'

Notably, the word 'andato' was gender specific. If a woman said she had gone for a walk, the word 'andato' would change to 'andata.'

I came to regard such gender variations as adhering to the Roberto Principle, and given Annika would be taking charge of our class again in a few weeks, I made a careful note of them.

After all, we didn't want another bloodbath.

Chapter 24

Short Stories

Most of us arrived for class brandishing a copy of Short Stories in Italian for Beginners - Volume One.

In addition to its clichéd cover illustrations and ubiquitous Vespa, there was a short body of text beneath the title:

Read for pleasure at your level and learn Italian the fun way.

The stories had been created and compiled by a fellow named Olly Richards.

I wouldn't be surprised if Olly were a member of the Duolingo explanation fraternity, as there were two words plastered on the front cover of his book that I immediately took exception to:

Beginners and Fun

According to its back cover, our new textbook contained 'an unmissable collection of eight unconventional and captivating short stories, carefully written to provide a sense of achievement and a feeling of progress when reading.'

Over time, all of that may prove to be the case, but we were on the verge of losing some of our original class members, and I was concerned that working through the stories in this new book would only accelerate that process.

In any case, the first story was titled:

La Pizza Pazza

Crazy Pizza

It was a curious concept, but after the tremendous success Carlo had enjoyed with his love potion minestrone, I guess anything is possible.

We took turns reading a couple of paragraphs in Italian before the next person in line would do their best to translate that same text into English.

La professoressa was working her way around the room in a clockwise direction, and I was quickly reconciling the order of students, to see if I was in line for the Italian or English element on the first rotation.

It was a relief to calculate that barring an unscheduled bathroom break, I would be reading the Italian text.

As much as it was jarring to see and hear others struggling with their translation, it was encouraging to think that when the time came, I wouldn't have to suffer the same fate, at least not the first time around anyway.

The first of four chapters introduced us to Daniel and his sister Julia. They were twenty-four and twenty-three years old, respectively. They were both students who lived in London with their parents, and they were flying to Rome for a vacation.

Julia confessed to being very anxious about the whole trip, as the only person she would know in Italy was her brother before her father gave them both some extra cash on the way to the airport, which helped to settle her nerves.

Each chapter had a brief summary, and we were tasked with reading it, translating it, and answering five multiple-choice questions relating to the text that preceded it.

By the time we had returned from la pausa, Daniel and Julia had arrived in Rome to be met by Daniel's friend Armando.

The three of them get into a taxi, and soon after they arrive at Armando's apartment, where Daniel and Julia both confirm that they are very hungry.

Armando explains that there are two restaurants close by. One is a trattoria that serves homemade pasta, and the other is a pizzeria called La Pizza Pazza.

Both are excellent options, but the two siblings will have to travel and eat alone, as Armando has a college lesson.

Daniel and Julia leave the apartment and ask for directions in the street. They discover that the best way to get to La Pizza Pazza is to catch the Number 35 bus, but it is late in the day and sure to be very crowded.

Julia doesn't particularly fancy cramming onto a bus with dozens of sweaty Italians, and suggests that she and her brother walk to la trattoria instead.

Daniel, who is clearly a bit of an idiot, suggests that he catch the bus to La Pizza Pazza, and that his sister walk alone to la trattoria. Once he arrives at la pizzeria, he will call her on his cell phone. That way, they will be able to discuss and compare both options.

What could possibly go wrong?

Daniel boards the bus and promptly falls asleep, before the driver wakes him up, having arrived in far-off Civitavecchia.

Daniel goes into a minor tailspin, retrieves his cell phone from his pocket, and tries to call his sister, only to discover that his phone battery is flat.

He then asks the bus driver if there is a public phone box nearby. The driver reminds him what year it is, and suggests he ask to use the phone in a nearby restaurant instead.

Daniel walks to the restaurant and is able to use the phone, but the moment he picks up the handset, he can't remember his sister's number.

We had all pretty much gathered the gist of the story by this stage, and at the very least, those of us who were tasked with translating a couple of paragraphs could make a calculated guess as to the words and phrases that outlined Daniel's dilemma.

Our hero then does what any sensible, clear-thinking, and mature adult would do in such a stressful situation.

He orders a pizza.

However, this does allow him to use the phone again, this time to call his mother in London.

Next week we will discover how Daniel's mother reacts, and what her dopey son decides to do next.

Chapter 25

One Down

Giuliana had been with us every step of the way. She had attended every Beginners Class the previous year and stuck with learning Italian when her own husband gave it away. She had come to the mid-year lunch at D.O.C. and our end-of-year celebration at Onde.

She also turned up to week four of Italian Two, but only to extend la professoressa the courtesy of saying she wouldn't be staying for the day's class, and that she wouldn't be coming back.

Giuliana had fallen victim to our second-year progression, and she was the first pin to fall.

I walked over when Bronwyn announced to the rest of the class that Giuliana had decided to leave.

I did my best to get her to stay, assuring her that many of us were finding things difficult and that she wasn't alone.

"I can't keep up, Michele," she said, shaking her head. "I'm just hopeless."

I dispensed with the Italianization at this point and protested, "Don't be ridiculous, Gill. You're not hopeless."

She looked at me, somewhat nonplussed and unconvinced.

"Now, Roberto," I insisted. "He was hopeless!"

It made her smile, but we never saw her again.

Given la professoressa would be away in Italy for the next two weeks, she wanted to make every effort to finish La Pizza Pazza before she left, so we broke with convention and made a start on the story prior to la pausa.

Daniel speaks with his mother on the phone. He explains the situation and asks that she call his sister and apologize on his behalf. He then finds a hotel, to spend the night, and so concerned is he about his anxiety-ridden sister's welfare that he wakes up and eats breakfast in his room at 10:00 am.

After checking out of the hotel, Daniel wanders outside, where he sees a truck parked by the roadside with the words, 'La Pizza Pazza' written on the driver's side door. Ever resourceful, he speaks to the driver, explains his dilemma, and asks him for a lift.

The driver is employed to make deliveries to La Pizza Pazza and agrees to give our hero a lift to la pizzeria. All the same, he insists Daniel ride in the back of the truck and remain unseen, with a load of tomatoes, cheese, and assorted condiments for company.

Grateful and relieved, Daniel quickly climbs into the back of the truck.

His journey has only just begun when he discovers a man hiding behind some of the many boxes of ingredients.

A conversation ensues, whereby the man begs him not to alert the driver to his presence, saying he needs to get to Rome, where he hopes to reunite with his son.

Daniel explains how he came to be in Civitavecchia and about his friend Armando. At this point, it turns out that the man hiding in the back of the truck is in fact Armando's father.

What are the odds?

A few hours later, the two protagonists arrive at La Pizza Pazza.

Daniel jumps out from the back of the truck to thank the driver, which gives the man who insists that he is Armando's father the opportunity to escape unseen, and together, they catch the Number 35 bus to Armando's building.

They knock on the door of Armando's apartment, but there is no answer, so Daniel retrieves a key that his friend had given him the previous day, and they both go inside.

Daniel manages to charge his phone, and after fifteen minutes, he calls his sister, who hurries back to the apartment with Armando in tow.

The two friends arrive thirty minutes later, at which point Armando immediately asks Daniel, "Who the hell is this guy?!" or words to that effect, anyway.

Daniel explains to Armando that the man he is with is in fact his father.

At this point, I felt sure we were about to learn the word for 'bullshit' in Italian.

In any case, the man explains that his name is Antonio Sottomente and that he is indeed Armando's father before he explains just how and why the two of them had been estranged for several years.

Eventually, Armando is convinced, and he suggests the four of them all go out to celebrate what has been a crazy couple of days.

Julia suggests they go to La Pizza Pazza, but Daniel objects, saying he doesn't want to catch the bus or hear the name La Pizza Pazza ever again.

Ultimately, they settle for a hamburger (as you do in Rome) before we wished la professoressa, 'Buon viaggio' for the next two weeks.

Chapter 26

The Bell Is Back

Most of us were on the lookout, or ear-out, for Annika's preferred attention-grabbing mechanism, but when she rang her little brass bell, it certainly caught some of the new brigade off guard.

It was down to business right from the outset.

I was impressed that Annika had remembered most of our names from the previous year and flattered that she had remembered mine.

Her preferred method of attack had always been to isolate a single student and 'invite' them to conjugate a particular verb of her choosing.

Sure enough, some of us were called upon to do just that, listing the 'I, you, he/she, we, you (plural) and they' elements of some common Italian verbs.

Those who were called upon all performed well. I, however, was spared, which was probably just as well, as I was no good thing to come through under that sort of pressure.

Annika then introduced us to modal verbs, listing three common Italian ones on the whiteboard.

Given that most of us hadn't been at school for several decades, it was helpful to be reminded that modal verbs express a desire, necessity, or possibility.

As she outlined each verb's conjugation, I scribbled a short sentence in my notebook, 'Voglio, posso, devo imparare l'italiano.' - I want to, I can, I must learn Italian.

I soon decided to focus on what Annika was actually writing and saying instead, as any minute she might turn the whiteboard around and obscure her presentation from view.

She could then call upon some unsuspecting student (for example, me) asking them to recite one of her freshly constructed conjugations.

Happily, this didn't happen, and secure in the knowledge that most of us had made detailed notes, she introduced us to various nuances of the Italian language.

She explained how certain verbs should precede others to indicate that something is happening in the present moment, and how asking someone, 'What..?' will differ depending upon if the subject of the question is a verb or a noun.

We were reminded of the curious gender change that eggs enjoyed when expressed as a single or plural, and we discovered that the same rationale applied to fingers, 'il dito' (masculine) for a single finger and 'le dita' (feminine) for more than one.

That ancient Roman scholar really should have asked someone to proofread his dictionary.

I chatted quite warmly with Annika at the break, and was able to penetrate her intense exterior, to learn something of her extensive teaching background and her love of languages.

We returned to class soon after, reminded how lucky we were to have such skilled and experienced instructors willing to volunteer their time each week.

The next few minutes were devoted to revision and a general question-and-answer session.

It was an exercise that made good use of someone who was a very experienced educator and entirely fluent in Italian.

With about half an hour remaining, we started a new chapter in the textbook that was appropriately titled - Giving Commands.

Giving commands uses the imperative tense, and in Italian, according to the textbook, 'The imperative is formed by dropping the infinitive ending of the verb, and then adding the relevant imperative endings according to the verb type.'

One of the great stumbling blocks I continued to endure throughout my Italian language journey was making sense of verb types and tenses.

Giving commands in the imperative tense was no exception.

Of course, if I should ever confess as much, some well-meaning classmate would invariably translate the Italian definitions of the present indicative, present perfect and imperfect for instance.

My problem wasn't so much their translation, as the fact that I couldn't be sure what those same terms meant in English, and I fear I wasted a tremendous amount of time and energy in class trying to decipher them, by which time I had invariably lost track of what we were talking about in the first place.

Eventually, I decided never to confess my ignorance ever again, as doing so would invariably invite a reply that was as confusing as it was condescending, and I didn't particularly want to fall out with anyone over something as trivial as a verb conjugation.

Chapter 27

The Emperor's New Clothes

For Thanksgiving, my aunt flew from Boston to visit me, my brother, and one of my late mother's oldest friends, who lived in Cobble Hill.

We met and strolled down Congress to Hicks Street one evening, where we had booked a table for dinner at an Italian restaurant.

From the moment we set foot 'nel ristorante,' our party was descended upon by an excitable, passionate, and theatrical cameriere.

He threw his arms out wide, elbowing my brother and me out of the way, while shouting enthusiastically, "Signora, signora, benvenuta!"

I couldn't be sure what he was saying after that, but it was clearly fluent Italian, as he indulged in every conceivable stereotype, while trying to impress and cajole two women in their eighties.

I was feeling a bit put out at the lack of attention that I had been afforded up to this point, and protested, "I'm the one paying for this, you know."

It didn't make the slightest difference, as il cameriere pulled out a couple of chairs, and ushered the two women into their seats, while my brother and I were left to fend for ourselves.

The floor show continued as he presented us with menus and explained 'i speciali' exclusively to the two women, amid a colorful flourish of language, and gestures.

The only time he interacted with me was when I tried to hand him the wine list.

I looked over my shoulder and reached around with the list, explaining that we wouldn't be ordering a bottle that evening.

"Don't worry about it," he said (in English), "I'll come and get it in a minute."

He could not have spoken those words in a more long-established and well entrenched New York accent.

The veil hadn't been lifted so much as disposed of, and the entire illusion he had so meticulously created was completely shattered.

Not that my aunt and our friend could care. They were having the time of their lives, lapping up every ounce of attention this clown could smother them with.

Orders were placed and plates delivered for the next hour or so, all presented with the usual theatrics before we enjoyed 'un dolce.'

Our host did his best to maintain his elaborate facade throughout, and when it came time to pay 'il conto,' I think even he was getting a bit tired of it.

To be fair though, the food was indeed 'delizioso' and I can certainly recommend the pumpkin and mushroom risotto.

By all means, check out Italy One for yourself.

Just don't take your girlfriend.

Chapter 28

Student Teacher

When la professoressa returned to class, she immediately told us about her near-miss exit flight at the airport.

She had arranged to fly to Italy with the frequent flyer miles she had accumulated with a particular airline and was expecting to enjoy an itinerary, that no doubt suited the airline and traversed half of Europe before her plane landed in Rome about two days later.

It wasn't until she checked in that she was alerted to a problem.

B. Street held her frequent flyer account, while her passport was in the name of Bronwyn Street.

Well, you can guess the rest.

Imagine the glaring oversight of a major international airline that would ensure it didn't have to honor free travel to an established and loyal customer because the name listed on her frequent flyer account differed ever so slightly from her passport.

It must be the oldest trick in the book.

As it turned out, the same airline had a direct flight to Rome, leaving in a few minutes.

After producing a credit card, paying the full fare, and breaking the four-minute mile en route to the departure gate, she boarded the plane in time.

The scholarship she had been awarded was indeed offered to teachers of Italian, but the course she was enrolled in was otherwise populated by students of the language. Most of whom, were nineteen-year-old Brazilian party animals.

She had survived the experience, however, and appeared to have enjoyed herself, as she encouraged us all to partake in an Italian drinking song, albeit with tea, coffee, and water, that she had learned in class.

The song had been created to recognize people's birthdays and was clearly designed to make a small group of people very drunk, very quickly.

Even the more philosophical elements of the course she attended were alcohol-related, as we were introduced to the popular Italian expression:

L'acqua fa male, il vino fa cantare.

Water makes you ill, wine makes you sing.

While she was in Italy, I wonder how many of her young Brazilian friends became familiar with the lesser-known expression:

Ma troppo vino fa vomitare.

Bronwyn then gave us a brief insight into contemporary Italian culture.

She set up a laptop computer and played us a thirty-second Italian television commercial for Nutella on YouTube. The ad celebrated that spoonfuls of the sickly chocolate and hazelnut spread would brighten anyone's day while enhancing or creating wonderful relationships. This is to say nothing of the fact that a

Nutella-based diet would 'apparently' provide a clear and uninterrupted pathway to lasting health, happiness, and prosperity.

The ad did introduce us to some useful words and worthwhile elements of the language, but for the most part, it demonstrated that the Italian advertising industry is just as capable of producing the same sort of mindless, puerile rubbish that we enjoy in this country.

Chapter 29

Paolo's Wine Tour

One of the new students to join our class was an outgoing, cheerful, and friendly wine broker whom we all knew as Paolo.

La professoressa had decided that we should continue our Italian Cultural Tour, and she invited Paolo to make a presentation the following week about Italy's various grape-growing and wine-making regions.

According to Paolo's map, the entire country comprised regions that grew grapes and made wine.

I counted twenty, which was a fair advance on what I knew, given the only Italian wine regions I could have identified before his presentation were Tuscany and...

Well, come to think of it, Tuscany was the only one.

The accompanying handout presented a written breakdown with further details of five regions in particular, a list of 'useful contacts,' and a directory of wineries that offered tastings, tours, and accommodation.

Paolo explained that many people who live on rural properties throughout Italy will welcome tourists into their homes, acting as local guides for what he called 'gastro tours.'

He claimed it was not uncommon for these same people to collect their guests at the local train station, before treating them to a sumptuous home-cooked meal, ahead of a few winery visits the next day.

He made the whole concept sound so appealing and enticing that it was all I could do not to surf a couple of websites during class, and I couldn't think of a more delightful circumstance to put some of my rudimentary language skills to the test.

In addition to Tuscany, some of Italy's more prominent wine-making regions include Piemonte, Veneto, Le Marche, and Abruzzo.

Piemonte rivals Tuscany in laying claim to being Italy's top wine-producing region.

A task made all the more difficult by the fact that before this day, I had never heard of it.

It was no surprise to learn that it bordered France, and as much as Piemonte 'sounds a bit French,' it means 'foot of the mountain.' The region's name simply reflects its location, at the base of the Alps.

Often called 'Italy's Burgundy,' given it is home to so many small vineyards, the Piemonte region is famous for growing the Barbera grape, which boasts classic Italian flavors, including sour cherries with high acidity.

East of Piemonte is the Veneto region, which, other than being home to the canals, gondolas, and massive cruise ships of Venice, produces more wine than any other region in the country.

The Veneto region is most famous for producing Prosecco, a sparkling wine made from the Glera grape, that many Italians argue should be afforded the same product and naming protections as Champagne.

The Marche and Abruzzo regions are located in the country's center, and are famous for the Verdicchio and Montepulciano grapes, respectively.

Le Marche's wine-making heritage dates back to Roman times, with some 60,000 acres of wineries operating today.

Abruzzo is directly south of the Marche region. It boasts a similar vintage and history, with more than 200,000 acres devoted to grapes and wineries.

Paolo then explained how and why each region's wines differed in style and taste.

Sicily's near-constant sunshine and reliable rainfall presented a vastly different climate and environment from areas that bordered France and Switzerland, while Sardinia's isolation varied the country's wine template even further.

With so much information having tantalized our taste buds, it was a shame that only coffee, tea, and water were on offer at the break.

After a brief chat during la pausa, we returned to class ready to tackle another riveting tale.

The next offering from Short Stories in Italian was:

La Creatura

The Creature

Judging by the title and an accompanying illustration of a remote cabin sitting on the shore of a lake, with a menacingly large animal footprint in the foreground, it promised to have a plot just as absurd and unlikely as that of La Pizza Pazza.

All the same, ours was a second-year Italian language class and not a collection of budding literary critics, so we pressed on.

We adopted the same strategy as before.

Someone would read a couple of paragraphs, having their pronunciation corrected throughout before the person sitting next to them would do their best to translate that same passage into English.

Once the process had circulated the entire class, we would reverse roles.

Today's story introduced us to Silvia, an adventurous and energetic young woman who was tremendously fond of the outdoors, and Giorgio, a more urbane fellow who was tremendously fond of Silvia.

The couple arrive at a remote lakeside cabin in the early evening, just as Silvia decides to share a rumor with Giorgio. She tells him about a mythical creature that roams the nearby woods, preying upon its unsuspecting victims, mostly at night.

Giorgio, while trying very hard to impress Silvia, dismisses the entire notion as 'ridicolo.'

Soon after, they open the door to the cabin, to find that it appears to have been uninhabited for some time. Then, they both hear a deep and menacing growl outside the back door. Silvia rushes toward a window, where she sees what appears to be a massive, black, bear-like creature disappearing into the woods.

Who's ridicolo now, Giorgio?

Chapter 30

Job Cards

The following week, we played cards, but not poker or blackjack.

We worked with a deck of cards that featured colorful illustrations of people engaged in their profession on one side, with a list of five job titles and subsequent explanations in Italian on the reverse.

The idea was to circulate the cards amongst class members, and for each of us to correctly identify which job title and explanation matched the illustration on the front of the card.

'La barista lavora in un bar,' matched the illustration of a smartly-dressed fellow presenting a customer with a cup of coffee in a café, for example.

La professoressa had kindly photocopied the reverse of all twelve cards, giving us a valuable future reference for some sixty professions.

Dopo la pausa, we returned to our short story and the remote lakeside cabin that Silvia and Giorgio were renting.

Having caught a glimpse of the mysterious creature, as it disappeared into the woods, Giorgio insists that he and Silvia separate and pursue it.

Silvia protests that Giorgio is 'pazzo,' but, excited at the prospect that, if he can snap a photo of the animal he may appear on television, there is no stopping him.

They both return to the cabin two hours later, neither having seen the creature. At which point, Silvia suggests they may have been the victims of a hoax.

However, the intrepid Giorgio will hear nothing of it and he sets out again, this time alone, determined to get a photo of the animal.

Before long, he stumbles upon a cave that he thinks may be the creature's lair and goes inside.

Checking his cell phone, he sees it cannot register a signal.

Several hours pass and Giorgio fails to return to the cabin.

After trying to call him several times and fearing her own phone may be defective, Silvia walks to a nearby village early the following day.

She arrives at a bar and asks to use the phone.

She then tries to call Giorgio several times to no avail.

Concerned, Silvia walks outside, takes a taxi, and soon after arrives at the cabin, where she can see a light shining inside.

Assuming that Giorgio has returned, she opens the door and calls his name.

There is no response, but as she enters, a group of her friends rush into the room, and jump out from behind the furniture, shouting, "Sorpresa!"

Silvia is taken aback and quite shocked, but she gradually collects her thoughts as her friends all applaud and wish her, "Buon Compleanno!"

A few minutes later, she catches sight of her mother, who is preparing some food in 'la cucina.'

Her mother explains that her father has been detained at work and that she doesn't know where Giorgio is, before the mysterious creature suddenly bursts through the back door of the cabin, and attacks her.

Silvia throws several punches and kicks out at the animal before realizing that it is in fact her father wearing a costume, and a mask, while Giorgio is filming the entire 'hilarious' episode on his phone.

Bruised, battered, and probably nursing a mild concussion, her father removes the costume and gleefully wishes Silvia a happy birthday.

I found the story positively underwhelming, but the exercise wasn't a complete loss, as we learned the phrase, 'C'è qualcosa che non mi quadra' means - There is something that doesn't add up to me.

An Italian translation for, 'This has to be the dumbest story I have ever read would have been more appropriate.'

Chapter 31

The Trickle Becomes a Flood

I t wasn't until we were given a handout titled, 100 Top Italian Adverbs that I realized how much I, and I feel sure several others, had learned.

I reckon I knew most of the words displayed, and the list clearly illustrated that English adverbs, that usually ended in - ly, were, for the most part, translated into Italian by simply adding - mente to the end of the original verb's stem.

Finally is 'finalmente' and probably is 'probabilmente,' for example.

Some of the adverbs on the list also featured within a series of common phrases and sentences that we spent the next few minutes translating.

After the break, la professoressa announced that those progressing from our Italian Two class would combine with her existing Intermediate Italian class next year. This would mean less time, effort, and responsibility for her, but more importantly, it was confirmation that we had progressed as far as we had and that (in her estimation at least) we were capable of joining a group of students who had been studying the Italian language for much longer than most of us.

However, I am not sure that Barbara was all that excited at the prospect of joining with the intermediates, given she emailed Bronwyn a few days later to say she was dropping out.

Barbara was one of the original beginners, and it was a shame to think we wouldn't see her again.

She cited the fact that she and her partner were renovating their apartment, as the reason she was leaving. Apparently, she wouldn't have enough time to focus on the project while keeping up with her Italian studies.

It didn't ring the least bit true to me, and when I contacted her myself the next day, she confessed that the various tense and grammar definitions we had been learning had finally proven too much, given she wasn't even sure what some of those same terms meant in English.

"Well, you are not alone there," I protested, adding, "I wouldn't know an infinitive preposition if it leapt off the page and hit me in the face!"

I did my best to get her to stay, suggesting that perhaps next year, a handful of us could sit together in a corner of the classroom reserved for the grammatically challenged.

Try as I may, however, she had made up her mind, and all I could do was wish her well, creating her 'nuovo appartamento.'

No sooner had Barbara left than Elena followed, and given Susanna had moved interstate, and Stefano hadn't shown up for months, we could now count the surviving beginners on one hand.

Five new students, who had started the Italian Two class that same year, had left by now, and the herd was definitely thinning.

At least there was no fighting over clean coffee cups during la pausa.

Chapter 32

Known Knowns and Known Unknowns

Next up, we were introduced to two new Italian verbs. Sapere and Conoscere.

Sapere is to know a fact or how to do something.

Conoscere is to have a general knowledge of something, or to be acquainted with a person or topic.

I would have liked to have seen former Secretary of Defense Donald Rumsfeld get his head around those two.

It would have been a press conference for the ages that one.

The next stop on our linguistic journey was 'partitivi' or partitives, another grammatical classification I wasn't sure how to define in English, let alone Italian.

Partitives are phrases that express a quantity or part of a noun distinct from its whole.

La professoressa then invited us all to make a 'partitive contribution.'

Paolo didn't surprise anyone, suggesting, 'un bicchiere di vino' - a glass of wine.

In contrast, others proposed cups of coffee and bowls of soup, with suggestions of 'una tazza di caffè' and 'una ciotola di zuppa.'

I suggested "un caso in punto," meaning - a case in point, I think.

I knew perfectly well that it wasn't correct, but I thought it was pretty funny, which, of course, at the end of the day is the main thing.

One of the convenient aspects of la professoressa's structured and ordered approach to teaching was that (provided she didn't start with me) I could generally work out which questions I was likely to be presented with, simply by counting the number of students ahead of me in our seating sequence and reconciling that number with the upcoming content of the textbook.

I daresay Bronwyn was simply trying to be fair and to ensure that everyone had an equal opportunity to contribute.

All the same, a bit of arithmetic usually gave me a head start in formulating an answer. Of course, if I was feeling reckless and brave, I could have looked the answers up in the back of the book ahead of time, but having called others out previously for 'allegedly' doing just that, waving my hand in the air while shouting, "Miss, Miss, Hooper's cheating!" I didn't want to take the risk of being caught myself.

Dopo la pausa, we started another short story titled:

L'Orologio

The Watch

The story promised to be more engaging, as its first page was flanked by an illustration of two people chasing what appeared to be a seventeenth-century pirate along a beach.

Our sequential reading and translation process gradually revealed that the story's central character was named Orlando. He was a watchmaker and repairer who lived and worked in Venice.

One day, he is walking along the beach with his friend Susanna when they come across an antique watch lying on the sand.

Orlando is fascinated, as he has never seen a watch like it before. He suggests that he takes it back to his workshop and that Susanna join him there in an hour.

An hour later, Susanna arrives to find Orlando very excited, as the watch appears to be in perfect working order.

In the meantime, the resourceful Susanna has been to the local library, and she presents Orlando with a book that has an illustration that looks exactly like the watch they have just found.

What's more, the watch in the picture is believed to have belonged to an infamous seventeenth century pirate named, Petar the Kraken.

And better still, the watch is rumored to have had magical powers.

Just then, Orlando and Susanna hear a noise in the back of the shop, and suddenly, a man (dressed oddly enough as a pirate) bursts in, grabs the watch, and runs off with it.

Orlando and Susanna give chase and manage to restrain the man, at which point an argument ensues as to who is the watch's rightful owner.

The 'Finders Keepers Argument' doesn't really resonate with the pirate, who insists that the watch belongs to him and that he is Petar the Kraken.

Just how an infamous and menacing seventeenth-century buccaneer was so easily overpowered by a Venetian watchmaker and his girlfriend might be explained, 'la settimana prossima' - next week.

Chapter 33

The Venetian Vortex

Before we could return to the shores of Venice and its time traveling pirates, we were introduced to the concepts of cardinal numbers, ordinal numbers, and fractions. Happily, algebra wasn't on the syllabus.

If nothing else, I learned that cardinal numbers were what most of us already knew as numbers - 'uno, due, tre,' for example.

Ordinal numbers define a position in a sequence - 'primo, secondo, terzo,' for example.

We had of course been introduced to ordinal numbers before, when la professoressa had confirmed the date.

Doing the shopping was a logical progression, and we were soon off to buy some food. Since I was now a veteran of the Duolingo experience, I was already well acquainted with the words for oranges, apples, and lemons, but I was soon shown up by some of my more experienced classmates, who proudly demonstrated they knew the Italian words for artichoke, cucumber, and grapefruit.

I could, of course, be consoled by the fact that I am never likely to buy any of those things anyway.

A trip to the delicatessen was a more complicated exercise, however.

I was relieved when we eventually moved on to a revision of clothing, as I was much more comfortable being presented with shoes, socks, and shirts than with a seemingly endless assortment of variations that defined a product I simply knew as ham.

Dopo la pausa, we returned to our short story, to discover that it really was the pirate Petar the Kraken standing in Orlando's workshop and that his watch did indeed have magical powers.

Susanna shows Petar the book she has borrowed from the library.

At this point, the pirate is delighted to discover he is famous. However, his joy is relatively short-lived, when Susanna points out that his watch is far more famous than he is.

Petar confesses to being amazed by all the tall buildings he can see when Orlando suggests that he and Susanna travel back in time with him to the seventeenth century.

At first, the pirate refuses, but when Orlando points out that Petar can only return because he and Susanna found his watch, he reluctantly agrees.

Moments later, the watchmaker and his girlfriend are standing on the deck of a pirate ship in the 1600s.

The ship's crew is familiar with such strange comings and goings, and pays them little heed, before Petar introduces them both to Filip, his second in command.

Filip immediately takes Orlando and Susanna aside and apologizes, explaining that they are about to be involved in a fierce battle with a fleet of ships from the Venetian Republic. What's more, it is a battle Petar's men cannot possibly win, as they are hopelessly outnumbered and outgunned.

Filip looks despairingly at Orlando and Susanna. He shakes his head and tells them Petar is 'positively pazzo.'

Orlando and Susanna realize that their only hope of escape is to steal the watch.

Still, Orlando confesses he is only a watchmaker, not a commando, and asks, 'How am I supposed to steal a watch from a pirate?'

Orlando seems to have forgotten that he and Susanna had managed to overpower Petar the Kraken once before, but in any case, Susanna has an idea.

With a vast Venetian armada gathering on the horizon, Susanna asks to look at Petar's watch, saying that she has an idea how he can be sure to win the battle.

Petar is guarded and looks at her suspiciously, saying, 'But you already know how the watch works.'

Susanna then explains that she and Orlando can transport Petar's entire ship and crew to another place and time, so there is no need for a battle.

The pirate is not interested, and he shouts at his crew to prepare for the fight.

Orlando demands to see the watch shouting, 'It is the only way you can win the battle!'

Just then, a Venetian cannonball hits the side of the ship, and Petar falls onto the surface of the deck.

Orlando seizes his chance. He grabs the watch and runs off, tossing it to Susanna as Petar shouts at his crew to stop them.

Just as Orlando runs towards Susanna, Petar is back on his feet, as cannon fire rains down upon the ship.

The pirate grabs Susanna and tries to wrestle the watch from her grasp. Filip and Orlando join the fray, and in the ensuing struggle, all four of them are magically transported to the Venetian foreshore in the twenty-first century.

Petar is the first to realize what has happened. He looks around for the watch, only to see it lying under Filip's foot, broken.

The pirate berates his second in charge, 'What have you done?! How are we going to get back now?!'

Filip doesn't reply. He is struck dumb by his surroundings and gazes in wonder at all of the tall buildings, and the odd cruise ship.

Susanna suggests they all return to Orlando's workshop, as he may be able to repair the watch.

Petar (who is remarkably calm and amenable) agrees.

Orlando agrees to repair the watch, but on the strict condition that Filip take charge of it and that it is destroyed the moment he and Petar the Kraken return to the seventeenth century.

Petar and Filip both agree that the watch is more trouble than it is worth.

A short time later, Orlando repairs the watch, and miraculously the two pirates return.

If Petar and his crew did manage to survive their battle with the Venetian navy, I reckon there is a fair chance Filip was fed to the sharks soon after.

That is if the Adriatic has any.

Chapter 34

Leocadia

The holidays were fast approaching, and la professoressa explained that she would be away traveling for the remainder of the year.

The school had made arrangements concerning a replacement, but that was all we knew.

We returned for the year's final few weeks, unsure what to expect, having been advised that Annika couldn't fill in during Bronwyn's absence, but also reassured that the school had everything in hand.

We were all sitting at our tables making polite and quiet conversation when a tall woman with shoulder-length brown hair appeared standing in the doorway.

She told us that the school had been in touch with her to ask if she could help us out for a few weeks, as a replacement instructor, but that she would only do so if we really wanted her to, and if we were all happy about it.

Everyone seemed delighted at the prospect, and we gave her a ringing endorsement as she entered the room.

She seemed reluctant to position herself in front of the class, and stood just inside the door, explaining something of her background.

Her name was Leocadia and she was the daughter of Italian immigrants who had settled in New York in the 1950s, before working in the construction industry.

One of us held up a copy of the textbook and explained what elements of the language we had studied to date, and where we were up to.

They didn't get very far.

Leocadia dismissed the notion with a polite, dismissive flick of her wrist.

"I am not interested in your textbook," she said. "You can put that away. We are going to engage in conversation."

An eerie silence followed as a dark cloud of apprehension and fear descended over the room.

"I want you to speak to one another in Italian, and ask questions of one another in Italian," she said.

"Then you will report whatever you have learned to the rest of the class in Italian. It doesn't have to be perfect," she added. "You just need to make yourself understood."

It was a prospect that had most of us both terrified and excited in equal measure.

However, in Emilia's case, it was probably more eighty/twenty.

Our first exercise was to team up with a neighbor and ask them to explain the nature and construct of their own family.

Whoever was asking the questions could take notes before the roles were reversed, and we would thereafter address the rest of the class, to explain the who's who of one another's family.

I teamed up with Linda and composed a series of questions that revealed she had two sons.

Their names were Jamie and Mitchell.

Jamie was the elder of the two and lived in Seattle.

Mitchell was a few years younger and lived in Los Angeles.

Neither had yet managed to present her with a grandchild and judging by the veil of disappointment that adorned her face as she shared that particular detail with me, it wouldn't be the worst thing if one of them did something about it before long.

Linda's Italian was more advanced than mine, and she fairly sailed through her questions, which, given the limited scope of my immediate family, didn't give her much to work with.

In any case, everyone did a good job with the exercise, as all the relevant information was presented to the class.

The tricky bit came when Leocadia herself decided to ask questions of students at random.

I was concerned that some of the more experienced among us would set the bar too high, and create an unrealistic expectation that the rest of us couldn't live up to.

Still, she was very patient and encouraging of us all, suggesting that several people in our class should be studying the language at a higher level.

Her approach was challenging, fun, and ultimately very satisfying, as it allowed many of us to retrieve hidden reserves of knowledge that were buried in the deep recesses of our memory.

Our compito was to link up with another student and draft a conversation that we would present to the class the following week.

The conversation could take place in a restaurant, a shop, or even under the auspices of a social outing.

All that Leocadia asked was that it not be boring.

Chapter 35

Conversations

Kaye and I teamed up to present la commedia that we had prepared during the week.

Our conversation was set in a shoe shop.

I played the role of a customer while Kaye was the shop owner.

Our exchange started out pleasantly enough, as the shop owner greets me and offers to help.

I tell her my size and point to a pair of shoes on display in the shop window, asking, "How much do they cost?"

Kaye manages to keep a straight face as the shop owner and replies that the shoes are 'on sale' and a bargain at, "Five hundred euros."

I reel back in horror and protest that five hundred euros for a pair of shoes is too expensive and that she must be pazza.

In response, the shop owner tries to justify the price, explaining that the shoes are handmade by members of a very famous family in Florence.

I reply, "I think that the family is perhaps more rich than famous."

The shop owner goes on to explain that the shoes are the cheapest ones she has in the shop, which pretty much puts an end to the pleasantries when I say, "I am sorry madam, but everything here is too expensive."

Before adding, "Dov'è la porta?"

I am not entirely sure why the customer felt the need to ask, "Where is the door?" having just walked through it moments before, but he says "Arrivederci" to the shop owner, and turns to leave.

As he does, the shop owner wishes him well, saying, "Buona fortuna, signore."

We have since learned that while 'buona fortuna' may well translate as 'good luck,' saying as much in Italy can be perceived as wishing someone the reverse.

Of course, in the context of our commedia, this was an inspired and quite brilliant riposte, even if it was a complete fluke.

To sincerely wish someone good fortune in Italy, it is more appropriate to say, "In bocca al lupo" - In the mouth of the wolf.

We learned that the expression 'In bocca al lupo' is often used in the theater and opera world, as performers wish each other well before a performance, rather like, 'Break a leg.'

However, many believe the expression originated centuries before amongst the hunting fraternity.

In any case, many people will say 'Grazie' in response. However, it is more appropriate to reply 'Crepi,' which is short for 'Crepi il lupo'- May the wolf die.

Kaye and I were first off the mark, before other presentations followed, consisting of conversations in restaurants, where specific dishes were recommended and drinks ordered.

Another took place in a train station, with a lost and confused tourist trying to figure out where she was, and how she was going to get where she needed to go.

Leocadia then created a scenario of her own. It was a situation she wanted a handful of us to act out for the benefit and amusement of the rest of the class.

She suggested that a small group of people arrive at a crowded and busy restaurant without a reservation, and for the restaurant owner/manager to be rather unhappy about it and very rude to them.

There are no prizes for guessing who landed the role of the restaurant manager.

I made as many notes as possible in the few seconds available, only to be reassured that I didn't need to make any.

Far from convinced, I put my pen down and did my best to live up to Leocadia's rather lofty and unrealistic expectations.

Kaye and Deborah led the charge as part of a group of five women who had arrived at the restaurant unannounced.

I was perfectly fine with our new instructor's direction that I be, 'abrupt and snooty.' In fact, I thought it all sounded rather fun. It was the process of enacting the role in Italian I was worried about.

Generously, Kaye and Deborah delivered an opening line that explained they would like a table for five people, but that they didn't have a reservation.

This allowed me to reply by repeating what they had said to me (amending it to express the appropriate plural verb conjugation of the word 'you') in an impatient and condescending manner.

They went on to confirm, 'We are all very hungry and happy to pay.'

I had learned the phrase and accompanying gesture, 'Me ne frego' in our first year, and at last I could use it in an appropriate (if terribly rude) context.

The customers then point to a couple of vacant tables, to which I reply, "I'm sorry, ladies, but I cannot help you."

This was probably the most polite thing I said during the entire discourse, and it brought an end to proceedings amid a warm round of applause from our contemporaries, and shouts of "Bravo!" from the most important person in the room.

Leocadia was very complimentary of the work that everyone had done, and she suggested that next week a couple of students volunteer to take charge of the class themselves and present whatever material they thought might prove relevant and worthwhile to the rest of us.

I felt quite sure that I had done more than enough for the time being, and I didn't dare say a word or move a muscle by way of volunteering before Deborah and Linda stepped up to the plate.

Chapter 36

Animals and Colors

As delightful and lyrical as the Italian language is, it has a very chauvinistic slant when it comes to the gender that various nouns possess.

I haven't done the math, but I am pretty sure that more Italian nouns are masculine than feminine, and some quite bizarrely so.

The word for brassiere, for example, is 'il reggiseno' and curiously masculine.

Generally, fruit, cities, islands, streets, sciences, and ships are feminine, but not bras. Work that one out.

Colors have their own rule book, and it was this topic that Deborah's presentation focused on the following week.

Colors are of course, adjectives, and their spelling and pronunciation will change depending upon the gender and plurality of the noun that precedes them.

'Una mela rossa' is a red apple, for example, while 'un libro rosso' is a red book.

If the apple and book are both pink, however, the spelling of the color itself does not change.

They would be 'una mela rosa' and 'un libro rosa.'

Other recalcitrant colors include blu and arancione. Not that anyone is likely to come across an apple that is either blue or orange.

The Italian language is awash with a great many exceptions. Most make about as much sense as men wearing bras, but there was little point in pondering or asking exactly why for students like us. It was a much more sensible strategy to accept 'that's how things are,' to remember the eccentricities as best we could, and press on.

Linda's presentation followed, and we were all asked to keep ourselves occupied for a minute or two as she busily prepared something on the reverse of the whiteboard.

Once she had finished, she called for everyone's attention.

She then turned the whiteboard around, where we could see that she had attached an 'alphabet of animal illustrations,' featuring individual pages torn from an Italian children's coloring book.

All twenty-one letters of the Italian alphabet were represented, with an illustration of an animal, bird, or insect whose name started with that same letter.

Our task was to collectively guess, decipher, and shout out each one.

A was for 'Ape' - Bee, while the letter B itself stood for 'Balena' - Whale.

As we progressed through the alphabet, we were encouraged to construct a short sentence that featured the name of each animal, which soon descended into a friendly argument when Linda insisted, "Tutte le balene sono grigie." - All whales are gray.

It was a shame that such a great idea had to be sidetracked by debate and ridicule, but I just couldn't let it go.

Linda usually sat next to me in class, while Leocadia occupied that spot during her presentation, which meant that I was obliged to engage in a series of short conversations with a fluent Italian speaker, as each letter and each animal was defined.

Happily, we adopted a theme whereby we would identify which animals were 'pericolosi' - dangerous, and which were not.

Sharks and hippos were most certainly pericolosi, while for the most part, cats and birds were not.

Dopo la pausa, we revisited pronunciation, as Leocadia explained that we should try to pronounce every letter in any Italian word, place a greater emphasis on the first syllable of each word, and how we should pronounce each vowel.

We were then instructed to interview our neighbors again. This time, we had to learn, and subsequently explain to the rest of the class, what they were doing on Christmas Day, what they would be cooking and eating, who they would be sharing the day with, and what gifts they might be giving or hoping to receive.

We all presented our neighbor's plans for Christmas, after which Leocadia was kind enough to share a delightful anecdote of her own.

The previous year, she and her young family had planned a trip to Windham Mountain for a few days either side of the big day. It was a prospect that her children were decidedly unhappy about, as they were concerned that Santa Claus wouldn't be able to locate them come Christmas Day.

Happily, she was able to reassure them that they had nothing to worry about, as she had contacted Santa herself, presumably by email, to confirm their schedule and location.

Santa had, in turn, advised her that he had the matter well and truly in hand.

It's just as well the North Pole has a decent Wi-Fi connection.

Chapter 37

Story Time

I don't recall many stories that were read to me as a child, with the exception of Harry the Dirty Dog.

For those unfamiliar with the story, Harry (a beloved family pet) is a predominantly white dog with a handful of black markings.

Harry runs off one day, embarking on a grand adventure. He rolls in a mound of dirt, buries himself in a pile of coal, and gets completely covered in all manner of filth.

Eventually, he returns home, where his heartbroken family adopts him as an entirely new dog. It is only when he is given a bath that his family is delighted to discover that their new dog is in fact Harry after all.

To finish off the year, Leocadia read us two children's fairy tales (needless to say, in Italian) and our collective task was to translate them throughout and follow along as she showed us various pictures relating to each story before turning each page.

The first story was, 'Cappuccetto Rosso' and the second was, 'La Gallinella Rossa.'

Many of us knew these same stories as Little Red Riding Hood and The Little Red Hen.

I was familiar with the plot of Cappucetto Rosso, but I had no idea when it came to La Gallinella Rossa, and I felt mildly put out when Leocadia told us that she had selected these two stories in particular, because everyone would know them so well.

I could recall that Cappuccetto Rosso visits her grandmother's cottage, only to find a conniving and menacing lupo sitting up in bed disguised as her nonna.

All the same, I had no recollection that the animal had actually devoured the old woman before the young ragazza arrived.

I completely lost track of the translation process at this point, as I tried to reconcile the fact, that this gruesome and vicious tale had been shared with millions of small children for centuries.

And to think, these days we worry about kids playing violent video games.

I daresay most people already know that things don't end too well for 'il lupo,' as a local woodsman (armed with an axe) uses him to decorate the walls of nonna's cottage before Cappuccetto Rosso cheerfully skips off home, to deal with the post-traumatic stress disorder that will no doubt plague her for the rest of her life.

All the characters in La Gallinella Rossa survive, but I still found the supposed 'moral of the story' disturbing.

For those who don't already know, a hen finds some seeds, and when all her farmyard friends refuse to help, she decides to plant them herself.

She then harvests some wheat, cuts it down, grinds it into flour, and bakes some bread, as her animal friends decline the opportunity to help her at every stage.

She then presents the bread that she has baked to the other animals, asking them if they would like to share it.

At this point, they all accept quite gleefully.

I felt sure that the hen would share the bread and the other animals on the farm might decide to contribute what they could. For example, the cow could offer some butter, while the dog fetches some strawberry jelly before the duck offers to wash the plates in a pond. But the hen digs her claws in, tells them all to get stuffed (more or less) and refuses to share anything.

Murderous carnivores and selfish, miserable poultry.

Is it any wonder Harry the Dirty Dog is a classic?

Chapter 38

What Now?

L a professoressa had arranged to combine her Italian Two, and Intermediate students into one class for the new school year.

Having completed the enrollment process during the holidays, most of us gathered in Meeting Rooms 1 and 2 at the Lifelong Learning Institute to meet our new classmates.

Paolo had dropped out, deciding instead to teach a Beginners Class in the company of a native Italian friend of his, which meant the intermediates and a handful of new students slightly outnumbered the Italian Two brigade.

Our new class numbered eighteen, but word had spread that, for personal reasons, la professoressa would not return to teaching for the time being.

We introduced ourselves to one another and chatted quietly, before a woman named Di Lewis strolled over from the office to address us all.

Di was the school's course coordinator. She explained the situation concerning Bronwyn's absence and told us that despite its best efforts, the school had not found anyone to take charge of our freshly minted class.

I am sure we all sat there thinking, "Well, what do we do now?"

A few moments later, we found out.

Di explained that our class could be listed and defined as 'Self Help.'

Still, for that to happen, one of us would need to volunteer and fulfill the instructor role until la professoressa returned.

The silence that followed was deafening, as no one so much as blinked.

I looked around the room at a sea of faces, some of whom had something of a teaching background, and most of whom spoke, wrote, and understood Italian better than me.

Di did the same. She then paused for a moment, no doubt hoping that someone might step into the breach before she raised the stakes.

"Well, if no one is prepared to take over as instructor," she said, "we will just have to cancel the whole class."

Still nothing.

It was the sort of hammer-blow ultimatum that I felt sure would motivate someone to volunteer.

After a time it did, as I raised my hand (having not really thought things through) and said,

"Okay. I'll do it then."

I am not sure if the news was greeted with feelings of absolute dread or casual indifference, but no one said anything, apart from Di, who asked me to stop by the office after class, so that I could be inducted and educated about taking student rolls, together with the process of collecting keys and whiteboard markers.

Once Di had left, I didn't dare stand up in front of the class.

I stayed in my seat, suggesting that for the time being, perhaps we could all work through the textbook in the same manner as we had been doing, and hopefully la professoressa would return before long.

Everyone seemed reasonably happy with the idea, and I suggested that we pick up from where the Italian Two class had left off the previous year. If that happened to be several pages short of where the intermediates were up to, perhaps they could treat the exercise as a worthwhile and helpful revision opportunity.

This was, of course, code for, 'This is what we are going to do, and if you people don't like it, well you are just going to have to deal with it.'

But to be fair, I didn't detect the slightest hint of protest.

I reassured everyone that la professoressa would be back soon and that all we had to do in the meantime was "to hold things together."

My role became one of coordination, as I invited each student in turn, to read a section aloud from the textbook, allowing others in the class to offer advice and suggestions, or to ask questions of one another.

At one point, I tried to highlight a mistake that one student had made, asking the rest of the class if anyone could identify and explain just where the individual concerned had gone wrong.

It didn't go over too well.

I was accused of 'channeling Annika,' and given that I had clearly overstepped the parameters of my new role, I sat quietly in my chair, feeling mildly admonished, while vowing never again to make the same mistake.

Chapter 39

Zooming

Classes at the school continued in the same vein for several weeks, with everyone contributing something, while a few people distributed articles, puzzles, and helpful website links via email during the week.

It wasn't long, however, before the Covid epidemic took hold.

We were soon locked out of the classroom, and forced to conduct classes via Zoom.

Working through the textbook didn't seem like such a good fit, and I was very anxious to make Zoom classes fun, so we amended our approach.

From this point on, students would present a short story of their own creation each week.

The idea was for everyone to write and read aloud a few paragraphs of simple Italian prose that others could understand, interpret, and ask questions about.

This concept later morphed into presenting a countdown quiz, whereby each of us would deliver as many as ten clues (which became progressively easier) inviting others to identify the name, object, place, or person that was the subject of each quiz.

I don't know if any of us learned anything much, apart from storing away some useful facts ahead of the next trivia night, but the process, 'met the brief,' in that it was relaxed, enjoyable, and it held things together.

I wrote each student's name on small sheets of paper and placed them all in the 'Hat of Destiny,' before drawing each name at random and inviting that particular person to contribute.

Zoom microphone etiquette soon became an issue, however, as we were often privy to telephone conversations with friends, instructions to pet dogs, and I certainly didn't need a detailed debrief of anyone's recent hip replacement.

We had a couple of Anti-Zoomers among us, and one or two others had left the class altogether.

For the most part, however, we managed to hold on to everyone for much of the year, before Linda suggested and arranged for us to involve a friend of hers.

Linda's friend was Marina Villani. She was the daughter of Italian immigrants who spoke the language fluently and was happy to help.

Marina was an artist whose preferred medium was glass, and she crafted beautiful and colorful creations of all shapes and sizes from her studio in New Jersey.

Marina agreed to 'sit in' during our Zoom classes, to answer any questions we may have, correct our inevitable errors in pronunciation, and provide an intelligent and experienced insight into the Italian language.

She had migrated to the United States with her parents when she was young and had learned to speak and read Italian at her local church while doing her best to disguise her ethnicity (mainly at school) lest she be teased and picked on.

Marina proved to be a great asset, and she arrived just as we needed an injection of energy and a change of scenery.

By this stage, we had reverted to presenting our own short stories each week, and I adopted a theme of 'Famous Villanis,' as a means of paying tribute to Marina's contribution.

As far as last names are concerned, Villani is to Italy what Smith is in much of the Western world, and the Internet revealed that there was no shortage of politicians, artists, historical figures, and film stars in the Villani clan.

The famous actress and sultry heartthrob, Sophia Loren topped a list that included mathematicians, writers, and poets.

Loren was born Sofia Villani in 1934. Who knew?

We all convened at D.O.C. in Greenpoint for an end-of-year lunch, and although it was too far for Marina to travel, Bronwyn was able to join us and confirm her intention to teach our class again the following year.

It was a welcome piece of news that she had been kind enough to share with me a few days before and suffice it to say, it went down tremendously well, a pranzo.

Chapter 40

Back in Town

We returned to classes in September, and la professoressa managed to pick up quite seamlessly from where she had left off.

The previous year had placed us in something of a holding pattern, but all the same, it was good fun, and importantly, we had managed to keep most of the group together ahead of a return to more serious endeavors.

We started the new school year by summarizing the various verb tenses we had learned.

La professoressa then outlined a sample future tense conjugation for the following verbs:

Prendere

Amare

Finire

These three verbs mean to take, to love, and to finish, and like all Italian verbs, they maintain the same spelling of their stem, with an array of variations and attachments, depending upon the specific tense of the verb itself.

It was a lot to learn, but to be fair, getting to know the stem of each verb gave us all a chance to decipher its meaning and guess the rest.

We read through all the future tense examples aloud and, in turn, before we were tasked with completing two written practice exercises in the textbook individually.

Completing the written practice was as easy as falling off a log for me, given, this year I found myself sitting next to a new student named Ann, who was already proving to be a great asset. She had a brain the size of a small planet, she had diligently completed the written exercises ahead of schedule, and she could boast the most impeccable and neat handwriting.

While others could concede defeat or shame themselves, by looking up the answers in the back of the book, all I had to do was casually glance to my right and copy what my neighbor had written.

However, I did have to confess once or twice when doing so necessitated her turning a page.

I did pay close attention to la professoressa's presentation all the same, and just as I thought I had this future tense caper under control, we were introduced to the future perfect tense, or in my case, the future problematic.

This tense enabled us to express phrases such as, 'I will have eaten before you arrive' and 'You will have left before I get there' for example, and each one had to be preceded by the correct conjugation of the verb Avere or Essere.

I participated in the oral practice and then carefully copied the answers from Ann's textbook, before filing the whole thing in the 'troppo difficile basket.'

Happily, we moved on to reading and talking about sports, and even though much of the language was entirely new, at least the context was familiar, which certainly helped.

There was an entire paragraph in the textbook that outlined Italy's passion for, 'il calcio' - soccer, and I learned the team that wins the Serie A championship gets to wear a distinctive emblem on their playing shirts the following season.

Italy's national soccer team is known as, 'gli Azzurri' - the Blues, as unsurprisingly, each player wears a blue shirt.

And who said you can't learn anything worthwhile from watching sports?

Dopo la pausa, we were introduced to some common Italian expressions that one of us had found on the Internet.

We had previously discussed, In bocca al lupo and were soon getting our collective heads around:

Hai voluto la bicicletta. Adesso la pedala.

You wanted the bicycle. Now pedal it.

I was grateful that no one had ever said those same words to me whenever I had complained about the complexity of verb tenses or the exceptions that various nouns possessed. After all, I had decided to hop aboard the Italian bicicletta in the first place. I may as well make a half-decent go of pedaling it.

Acqua in bocca.

Water in mouth.

This is a way of telling someone to keep something secret, or at the very least, to keep the information to themselves. The idea is 'Don't spill the beans,' or in this case, don't let water spill from your mouth.

Non vedo l'ora.

I don't see the hour.

This expression means 'I cannot wait to see, have, or do something.'

Essere in gamba.

If someone wants to express the fact that another person is well-informed or in good shape, they might use the expression, 'Essere in gamba.'

No doubt, 'to be in leg' is a good thing. Exactly how or why that is, I have no idea.

Non mi va.

This expression translates as 'It doesn't go with me.'

It's a phrase that can politely decline an offer someone has made to you.

Essere in alto mare.

This phrase is used when someone is procrastinating or has some way to go before finishing a project, like writing a book for example.

Translating literally as 'To be on the high seas,' it means you still have a long way to go before finishing.

Non avere peli sulla lingua.

Don't have hairs on your tongue.

This phrase means to be straightforward and speak your mind clearly and directly.

I am tipping people say this one a lot in Italy.

Mangia bene, ridi spesso, ama molto.

This has to be everyone's favorite. It means, 'Eat well, laugh often, love a lot.'

If there is an expression that better sums up Italy's culture, its people, and the Italian way of life, I have yet to hear it.

Chapter 41

A Few Weeks Off

The end of the textbook was in sight, but there was no letting up regarding the complexity of verb tenses, as we were introduced to the conditional and past conditional tenses.

The conditional tense would allow us to say phrases such as, 'Uscirei stasera ma devo studiare' - I would go out this evening, but I have to study.

While a sample phrase in the past conditional tense might be, 'Ieri sera, ho provato studiare il mio libro di testo italiano, ma mi stava facendo impazzire' - I tried studying my Italian textbook last night, but it was making me crazy.

It was just my luck that we had struck upon a particularly tricky element of the language just as I was scheduled to miss a few classes.

I spent a week in the hospital, having what my surgeon described as 'a massive hernia' repaired, before recovering at home, and placing my all-in-one home gym and cause of said hernia, on eBay.

Linda was kind enough to visit me in a postoperative ward, bringing me a cup of coffee, a cookie the size of a Frisbee, and a copy of an Italian-language newspaper, while Kaye generously drove me to and from class for a few weeks after that.

Not wanting to be a burden, I insisted on driving myself before long, which didn't end too well on my first try.

As the parking lot was emptying after class, I could be seen contorting my recently tortured abdomen, while struggling to get into, and subsequently out of the car when my foot became wedged under the brake pedal.

I spent several minutes striking a rather unflattering pose, unsure if the best option was to press on or to bid an awkward and clumsy retreat before trying again.

I tried both a few times to no avail, but happily I had demonstrated enough sense to park at the end of a row of cars, and next to a strip of grass when I arrived.

The idea was to swing the driver's side door wide open, so that I could get out of the car in the first place.

This time around, however, even with the door at full stretch, the reverse procedure was proving to be a more difficult proposition, and I spent no small amount of time sprawled across the grass while trying to free my foot, without quite literally, spilling my guts, as I weighed up what to do next.

Eventually, I was able to free myself and retrieve my leg from the foot well.

I firmly clung to the door frame and hoisted myself upright, before executing a second (crude but effective) entry process to find myself seated behind the wheel.

It was no mean feat and a tremendous relief.

All the same, it was some time before the pain had subsided enough for me to even consider driving, and I was certainly grateful that I wouldn't need to stop anywhere to fill up with gas in order to get home.

I showed up again the following week to be mildly admonished by my classmate Dianne, who appeared somewhat concerned, as I gingerly shuffled across the parking lot, slowly wobbled down a set of steps, and made my way toward the classroom.

"Should you even be here, Michele?" she asked.

Dianne was a very kind and gentle woman, and I felt sure that she was expressing a sincere and genuine concern for my physical welfare.

All the same, I couldn't ignore the fact that her remark may well have been a thinly veiled swipe at my language skills.

Chapter 42

Eating Out

By this stage, a few of us had been circulating some additional learning material, puzzles, and website links that we could study between classes, and one such example was a document titled, 'Cosa Prendiamo?' - What will we take/have?

Cosa Prendiamo? explained that a meal in an Italian restaurant would typically consist of at least four courses:

Un Primo Piatto - often a soup or pasta dish.

Un Secondo Piatto - often meat, poultry, or fish.

Un Contorno - a side dish or salad.

Un Dolce - a dessert dish of fruit, cheese, or ice cream.

While a glass or two of a local 'vino rosso o bianco' would enhance and complement any meal.

The document detailed how some of Italy's many regional dishes were prepared, explaining the various combinations and sauces that might accompany an array of pasta dishes, for example.

It even included a couple of sample scripts that presented typical conversations between 'un cameriere' and a collection of hungry diners who had just arrived 'al ristorante' and sat at a table.

The menus and descriptions in the document painted a delightful picture of Italian couples and families dining in charming local restaurants, enjoying any number of delicious local delicacies, all of which were largely and sadly spoiled by the color photograph that sat at the top of the page.

The photo that accompanied the various articles, showed an overweight, balding, and clearly very hungry middle-aged man.

He was sitting alone and leaning over a table that was draped in a red-and-white checked cloth. A glass and a bottle of wine could be seen in the foreground, standing to one side of an ashtray that housed three or four cigarette butts.

Directly beneath the man's chin was a bowl of spaghetti, and seemingly oblivious to the presence of a camera, he was shoveling an enormous fork load of the stuff into his mouth.

In his left hand was a spoon, the tip resting at the bottom of the bowl. The spoon appeared cocked and loaded, ready to gather another massive portion of pasta that our ravenous diner would twist around his fork, before further feeding his face.

The photo completely belied the aesthetic that 'Cosa Prendiamo?' had created.

It looked like this guy hadn't eaten for weeks, and the photo could well have been captioned with a quote that read, 'It's the quantity I look for in a meal, not just the quality.'

All the same, 'Cosa Prendiamo?' motivated several of us to share some of our own Italian restaurant experiences.

Kaye told us that she saw a small poster displayed at D.O.C. in Greenpoint, advertising a series of dinners branded, 'Tastes of Italy.'

The idea was that twenty people would convene in a separate function room and enjoy a set menu dinner, featuring various traditional Italian dishes, each of which included ingredients and wines from specific regions of the country.

She and her husband first attended 'Tastes of Puglia,' which featured a delicious four-course meal.

Different wines accompanied each course, and from all reports, it was a challenge to consume everything on offer.

Tastes of Puglia, was followed two months later by 'Tastes of Abruzzo,' then Calabria, Le Marche, and Veneto, before Emilia Romagna rounded out the year.

A key element in each presentation was that the head chef would explain the various aspects of each menu to all of his guests before they were presented with their meals.

It was no surprise to learn that the food was excellent and the wines superb, while the chef's English improved significantly over the course of the year.

My own recollection was having dinner at a restaurant called, 'Ciao Bella' in Williamsburg, with a friend who was visiting from Australia.

I had chosen the restaurant specifically, and as the evening drew to a close, I was trying very hard to impress her by showing off my new language skills.

We had enjoyed a wonderful meal, and as the last of our plates were being cleared away, I thanked our raven-haired and olive-skinned waitress in my very best Italian.

I told her that we both thought her service was 'eccellente,' and the meal 'delizioso,' with a carefully scripted speech that I had been rehearsing for several minutes.

Having exhausted my modest reserves of Italian, I finished with a colorful and relevant flourish, presenting her with the time-honored gesture of twisting the tip of my index finger into my cheek.

"I'm from Egypt," she said.

Chapter 43

Unknown Lands

One of our more enthusiastic contributors when it came to distributing additional material, was a woman named Pam. She had come across a website devoted to students of Italian, and she sent us various files and website links where we could download and print numerous articles to read aloud in class, and have a go at translating.

One of her offerings was titled, 'Le Vacanze della Torre Eiffel.'

It told a very lighthearted tale of how the Eiffel Tower had decided to take a vacation in Italy.

La Torre traveled far and wide across the country, visiting Florence and Venice, before deciding to settle in Rome.

This created something of a diplomatic incident when the mayor of Paris called his Roman counterpart and demanded its immediate return.

A subsequent offering was titled, 'Gomorra,' and it was anything but lighthearted.

The article was a factual exposé that explained how criminal syndicates bribe, cajole, and threaten local councils and authorities, to allow them to illegally dump toxic waste all over the country.

The practice is rife in Italy, with specialist 'waste brokers,' operating lucrative businesses, acting on behalf of incinerators and manufacturers, while they in turn deal with corrupt local officials and chemists, who think nothing of falsifying documents if there are a few euros in it.

According to the article, there isn't a corner of the country that has been spared.

It was all rather depressing to picture a gorgeous Tuscan landscape, thinking that just beyond the horizon, there may well be a hidden landfill, housing a toxic time bomb that might one day poison the entire region.

I was grateful when we returned to some of the unrealistic fiction presented by Short Stories in Italian, as we worked through a rollicking narrative of ancient Viking explorers titled:

Terre Sconosciute

Unknown Lands

The first character we met was named Thoric. He was a mild-mannered family man who largely belied the Viking stereotype. He lived in a small seaside village bordered by snow-capped mountains and surrounded by land that was not particularly fertile.

The story begins just as Thoric has returned from a hunting trip. But before he can present his wife with the spoils of his endeavors, he is summoned to a meeting with Eskol, the village chief.

Eskol announces that there is a shortage of wildlife to hunt in the area, and it is too difficult to grow crops on the side of the mountains during the winter months in particular.

Therefore, he has decided that he and his most trusted followers will undertake an expedition to search for more fertile lands across the seas to the west.

The villagers are skeptical, as the male folk are conscripted to build a fleet of ships.

At the same time, Thoric is tasked with overseeing their construction.

As it turns out, Thoric's job isn't a particularly straightforward one, as he faces constant intrusion and pressure from Eskol, who is keen to set sail as soon as possible.

Not short on confidence, Eskol tells the villagers that he is certain more fertile lands lie to the west.

Excited at the prospect of finding and farming more food, the naive and optimistic villagers eventually throw their support behind the expedition.

Three new ships set sail two months later, with the ever-assertive Eskol at the helm.

Less than a week into the voyage and having lost sight of their lands, the ships are caught in a powerful storm that blows them off course, but Eskol insists they continue, sailing further and further west at all costs.

Several days later, there is no land in sight, and the crews are starting to worry, when a lookout yells at the top of his voice, waking a sleeping Eskol.

Given the nature of some of the other stories in the book, I half expected the sighting to be an alien spacecraft hovering above the fleet before it beamed some of the crew members aboard.

It was, however, 'un uccello' - a bird and a sure indication that land is close by.

Sure enough, there is a strip of land on the horizon, and the three Viking ships are soon anchored off a long, sandy beach.

Eskol directs his men to wade ashore before he orders them to split into small groups to hunt and find whatever food they can in the nearby forest.

The men set up camp on the beach that night, as Eskol decides they will explore the new land at dawn.

The next day, as the men are eating the spoils of their hunting endeavors, Thoric speaks with Eskol, asking him how he could be so sure that they would find this new land to the west.

Eskol tells Thoric that he had a premonition some months before, but he offers no reassurance as to how he and his men will find their way home, given they were hopelessly blown off course in the first place.

However, that issue is put to one side for the moment, as Eskol calls his men to attention and commands them to march into the forest.

The fearless Vikings mindlessly follow their leader and trudge through the dense undergrowth for several hours, before they come across a patch of open ground that contains a small village.

Eskol's men stand stunned and silent.

All of the villagers have long brown hair and very dark skin. They are wearing strange clothes and speaking a most bizarre language.

Not Italian, presumably.

At first, the villagers are afraid to see the Vikings standing at the forest's edge, as Eskol steps forward, calling upon his men to follow him.

Eskol raises his hand, trying to reassure the villagers that he and his men mean them no harm when a village elder steps forward.

The older man is understandably shocked to see and hear a bunch of sweaty Scandinavian mariners speaking Italian, given he probably understands about as much of the spoken language as me. All the same, he offers Eskol his hand and a drink of water.

The two men sit together and gradually come to an understanding, as the village elder explains to Eskol that he and his men are not the first foreigners to have come across their settlement.

Sadly, the last time a bunch of exotic travelers had shown up, a long period of illness followed, with many villagers succumbing to terrible sickness and dying.

Even so, the village elder extends a welcome to the Vikings, offering to help them assimilate with his people, and promising to teach them how to hunt for food and grow crops.

Eskol addresses his men, suggesting that they stay in this new, fertile land, rather than take the risk of navigating and sailing their ships back home.

The idea doesn't go over too well with most of them, but a handful, including Eskol himself, decide to stay, while Thoric takes command of the three ships and charts their return.

We never did learn if Thoric and his friends made it home.

Still, an addendum to the story explained that scientists have uncovered ample evidence to confirm that Viking explorers did in fact settle among the native populations of Newfoundland, Canada, in the eleventh century.

Chapter 44

Zooming Back

Some of us were anxious to further our conversation skills, and Linda in particular was often scouring the Internet, searching for tutorials and exercises offered by native Italians and fluent speakers.

She never found anything that seemed quite right online, so four of us decided to establish a conversation group of our own.

The idea was to meet for coffee after class and to only speak to one another in Italian.

The All Stars (as I dubbed us) first met at D.O.C. in Greenpoint during a mid-year break from school.

Given D.O.C. was as authentic an Italian ristorante as we could find, and most of its staff and some of its clientele were native speakers, it seemed like an ideal fit.

Linda, Kaye, Ann, and I gathered at an outdoor table on the terrace to enjoy a coffee, or in Ann's case, a cup of tea. At the same time, those seated nearby were 'entertained' by our clumsy language skills, awkward pronunciation, and appalling grammar.

Fortunately, our cameriere (a bright and cheerful young Italian fellow) was only too happy to indulge us.

I suspect he would have hung around much longer and probably pulled up a chair, if not for the fact he had more important things to be getting on with.

As he left us, he gestured to a man sitting at an adjacent table.

"This guy is Italian," he said. "He might be able to help you."

Suffice it to say, the man seated at the neighboring table was less than impressed that he had been drafted into the role.

He looked up from his newspaper, curled his lip menacingly, and waved his hand in the general vicinity of our waiter, snarling, "Ah, scusa!"

I marveled at the tremendous efficiency and economy of language he was able to demonstrate.

Executing a single (albeit elaborate) hand gesture, while uttering what was in effect just one word, he was able to communicate the phrase, 'What are you kidding?! I am trying to read the newspaper here. What do I want to help these idiots for? Leave me alone.'

Extraordinary.

We battled on regardless, and to our neighbor's credit, he did wish us all good luck a short time later, once he had finished his coffee, tucked his newspaper under his arm, and stood up to leave.

The All Stars only met on two further occasions before further COVID outbreaks rendered face-to-face classes off the agenda altogether.

Our class had no choice but to get together via Zoom again, this time with la professoressa at the head of proceedings.

We did, of course, have our textbook to work through, and Bronwyn called upon each of us to contribute in turn, as she normally would.

But for the absence of a whiteboard, it wasn't altogether different.

Happily, most of us managed to log on and show up each week, as I adopted the tactic of attending class via a laptop computer.

At the same time, my desktop PC was connected to the Italian category of Google Translate. It was the twenty first century equivalent of looking up the answers ahead of time, and if I were ever asked to present the class with a challenging translation, I would glance ruefully to one side and appear to be in deep thought, as I furiously attacked the keyboard of my PC.

Others in the class continued to make worthwhile contributions by emailing various articles, word puzzles, and crosswords ahead of time.

I am no great shakes when it comes to crosswords at the best of times, and it was frustrating to struggle with a solution to a clue that moments before had been introduced as, 'Oh, this is an easy one.'

All the same, if the crosswords were difficult and frustrating, Ann's 'What's Wrong?' exercises were infuriating.

Ann had almost certainly, topped a Beginners Class a year or two before, while she, her teacher, and a handful of other graduates still got together most weeks, as a kind of study group.

Their teacher occasionally provided her students with an exercise of her own creation - a list of twenty short sentences written in Italian.

Each student's task was to find the deliberate spelling and grammatical mistakes that all but one of the sentences contained, while identifying the single sentence that was in fact correct.

Each attachment was titled, 'What's Wrong?' as was Ann's email to me when she suggested that I circulate the list to everyone in the class.

I changed the title of the document and the subject of each email to, 'Spot the Mistakes,' as I didn't want to suggest to anyone that they might be on the verge of an emotional breakdown.

Other than me, that is.

Chapter 45

The Chaos of Pronouns

We had spent a considerable amount of time learning how to construct, translate, and respond to various sentences and questions, and now we could develop the capacity to present those same elements in a more conversational context.

Rather than say, 'Marco is reading the book now,' we could for example say, 'Marco is reading it now.'

As welcome and as realistic as it was to construct such a simple sentence, sadly, it wasn't as easy as it first appeared.

We read through all of the oral practice examples in the textbook, before studying the various forms of the third person direct object pronoun - possibly the most elaborate introduction that the word 'it' has ever enjoyed.

True to form, the English words, 'it and them' would translate in Italian as 'lo, li, la, or le,' depending upon the gender and quantity of the subject being referred to.

I had almost lost count of the number of variations before we were introduced to the concept of double, attached, and stressed pronouns.

For example, the use of an attached pronoun would allow us to say, 'Non posso capirlo' - I don't understand it.

At least, I think it does anyway.

We worked through the examples in the textbook, where people were buying shoes for one another and putting jackets on.

In contrast, others would confirm that they did this or that yesterday, or that they intended to do so soon.

Happily, things started to come together once we practiced presenting things to one another.

We worked our way around the class for the next few minutes, giving each other pencils, books, and pats on the back.

La professoressa then asked us to construct three short sentences that included both direct and indirect object pronouns.

Double, attached, and stressed pronouns were an option if anyone wanted to show off.

A few minutes later, I had the opportunity to present my own compilation:

Non l'ho fatto io.	I didn't do it.
Nessuno mi ha visto farlo.	Nobody saw me do it.
Non puoi provare niente.	You can't prove anything.

Ever diligent and professional, la professoressa marked me down because my third sentence didn't actually contain a direct or indirect pronoun.

"Yes, I know," I said, adding, "but that wouldn't have been funny."

It was simply a matter of priorities.

Apparently, entire books have been devoted to the subject, and when la professoressa confessed that Italian pronouns could be "a bit tricky," I think many of us took that to mean 'nigh on impossible.'

Compito for the week was to complete two different written practice exercises in the textbook and to tackle a test at the end of the chapter.

I had never been so grateful that the answers were printed in the back of the book.

Chapter 46

The Last Supper

The school year was drawing to a close, and la professoressa suggested that we all go out for lunch to mark the occasion of our last class.

Organizing the event largely fell to me, and I emailed everyone, asking them to suggest a suitable (preferably Italian) venue.

We settled on a restaurant called Donato's in Greenpoint, owned and operated by 'tre fratelli italiani' - three Italian brothers.

Donato's proved a popular choice, given it grew many of its ingredients in a garden that was located on-site.

The lunch was preceded by a contest to find which student had the most interesting middle name.

Ultimately, an expert panel (that is to say me) whittled the entries down to a shortlist of finalists.

Everyone who didn't make the final could vote 3, 2, or 1 (in a kind of MVP context) for those who did before the winner was presented with a prize, while we enjoyed a post-lunch coffee.

Elizabeth Jewel Armstrong was first past the post, with Joan Cecelia Lynch and Georgina Irenes Simmons tied for second place.

Given that none of us had any real control over our middle names, I decided that everyone should win a prize for having achieved something significant over the course of the year.

I had rewarded some of my fellow students similarly before and had kept a list of those who had earned a prize for correctly interpreting one of my submissions or for having laughed at one of my childish jokes.

I also rewarded the runners-up in the middle name contest, before creating some entirely new and obscure categories that allowed everyone to win something.

Ann qualified as she let me copy the answers she had neatly written in her textbook each week, while Vicki was included as a nod to the British Royal Family, having been named Victoria Elizabeth. While all Graham had to do was show up, to address a significant gender imbalance in the class.

We ordered a bunch of flowers for la professoressa, with the specific instruction that the bouquet be colored entirely green, white, and red. At the same time, Emilia offered to bring a card featuring one of her paintings that we could all sign.

Kaye was kind enough to give me a lift to the restaurant (via the florist) and we arrived a few minutes early arranging for the flowers to be stored in the office, while sixteen packets of M&Ms were housed in the fridge.

The restaurant seated us all at a single, long table, where I could sit diagonally opposite la professoressa, just out of range if I should be foolish enough to order a latte again.

After lunch, we presented Bronwyn with her flowers, just after I received a card that everyone had signed, together with a bottle of wine - a very generous reward for someone who had done little more than send a handful of emails throughout the year.

The event was a lot of fun and a great success. A glowing testament to the relaxed and friendly atmosphere that la professoressa had created and maintained throughout her tenure.

By this stage, I had developed a reasonable understanding of Italian grammar and a vocabulary that, while limited, was arguably enough to get me into or out of trouble if such an occasion presented itself.

In any case, it was time for me to take the next step, putting what I had learned, studied, and rehearsed in recent years into practice - an opportunity to subject any number of native speakers to my clumsy grammar and awkward pronunciation.

I would fly to Italy and spend a couple of months immersed in the country's glorious language and wonderful culture while doing my best to avoid the sights and paths so well and long worn by generations of tourists.

My plan was to avoid the larger cities and stay in more regional areas (where English is rarely spoken) while doing my best to understand and be understood without causing too much confusion or offense.

And just for good measure, I would take my textbook to study on the plane.

Chapter 47

Preparations

I was lucky to have two valuable resources to call upon before my departure.

These were my friend Brendan and a native Italian fellow named Franco, who la professoressa had enlisted to perform an assistant instructor role with our weekly language class.

Franco's role was ostensibly to point out and correct the errors that any of us made with our Italian pronunciation, and in my case, to diagnose a severe case of 'accent blindness,' when I failed (repeatedly) to properly emphasize and accentuate vowels at the end of words that sported such embellishments.

Born and raised in Verona, Franco was also able to educate us about Italy's various cultural nuances, and its many regional variations.

As much as I was fascinated to learn about the delicacies and dialects of individual areas, cities, and towns, I took particular note of one element of his Italian cultural exposé.

"Keep your hands on your money, passport, and credit cards, and never let go of your luggage."

It left me with the impression that stealing from tourists is something of a national pastime in Italy. If only one that is enacted by a small and nefarious element of the population.

Franco insisted that I buy a money belt that I could house beneath a shirt, if not tuck inside the waist of my trousers.

The idea was for it to contain my passport, credit card, and cash, as these things should never be housed in a pocket or left in a hotel.

When it came time to secure the appropriate adornment, I invested in one made from a fabric that would block anyone's ability to scan the microchips in my passport or credit card (while I was wearing it and while those elements were safely contained therein) as rather frighteningly, that's a thing nowadays.

My friend Brendan wasn't a member of our language class, nor was he a native Italian.

He is, however, a very clever guy, an engineer, and, together with his wife, a very experienced and seasoned traveler.

One day over coffee, I was trying to reconcile the fact that while I was happy to take my cell phone with me to Italy (if only to access the Internet and the odd SMS message) I didn't particularly want to come home to a $10,000 phone bill, and I would need to purchase and insert a local SIM card, to use the phone's GPS function, if I wasn't able to access a free Wi-Fi connection.

It was a curly and frustrating conundrum, as the only viable solution appeared to be swapping SIM cards in and out of my phone, or using an old second phone with a local SIM in the hope that the GPS application would be more or less up to date.

I pictured myself wandering the narrow, cobbled streets of Sulmona and Bari, not to mention the bustling metropolis of Rome or Milan, while swapping phones and trying to secure an Internet connection, all the while dealing with the inevitable and inescapable fact that I was almost certainly lost - again.

I couldn't see a way around the problem, let alone a solution, and I had resigned myself to the fact that I would be constantly asking local people for directions, across all parts of the country and at all hours of the day.

You can imagine my embarrassment when my friend suggested that rather than wrestle with two cell phones, two SIM cards, and various facets of telecommunication and GPS technology, that, perhaps I should invest in a map.

PART TWO

Italia

Chapter 48

Malpensa

My plane landed in Milan at 7:45 pm.

Milan was the destination where my travel agent had secured me the best deal on the cost of a flight, and I can remember dismissing its exact location with a flick of my wrist, as we sat either side of her desk.

At the time, I thought to myself, "Italy's not a particularly big country, and Milan is somewhere just north of Rome."

For others who may be equally 'geographically challenged,' Milan is actually quite a long way north of Rome and quite close to the Swiss border.

It is Italy's second-largest city, the country's economic powerhouse, and the beating heart of the world's fashion industry.

According to my Italy travel guide, any number of European aristocrats, Arab princes, and countless Hollywood celebrities choose to call Milan home.

So I should fit right in then.

I joined a steady stream of people following the overhead signs directing them to Passport Control.

Once we had reached its vicinity, I could see several large, arrow-shaped signs stuck to the floor.

One directed Italian and EU passport holders to one section, while, 'all other nationalities' were guided to another.

I was soon presented with a long, largely stationary queue of people, snaking its way inside a square-shaped construct of stainless steel poles and retractable tape.

Three women (all smartly dressed in navy blue uniforms) were directing more and more people to join the queue.

"Americani, Inglesi," one would say aloud, as another gestured to a gap in the sequence of poles and tape where new entrants could tack on.

As I approached, one of the women spoke to me directly, repeating the same refrain, "Americani, Inglesi," while extending her left arm and inviting me to join a queue, that, though shaped like a serpent, was moving at the pace of a snail.

I replied, "No, io sono australiano."

"Ah, questo," she said, pointing beyond the perimeter of the queue construction.

I pointed to it myself, asking (in English) "You want me to go this way?"

One of her colleagues then walked across, gestured along the outer edge of the queue box, and said, "Si, certo."

I wasn't about to argue, and I walked along the outer rear section of the box.

I turned left and then left again before I found myself standing in front of a booth that housed two men (who were both inspecting passports) and ahead of a queue of people that by now numbered at least two hundred.

I stood there for a few seconds before a vacancy opened, and another uniformed woman (standing at the head of proceedings) held her hand up very firmly to whoever was next in line.

She said nothing but pointed at me and then at the newly available inspector, clearly indicating, 'You, there, now.'

I was delighted to have jumped the queue, and presented my passport to the immigration official, together with an enthusiastic and clearly audible, "Buonasera."

He wasn't the least bit impressed.

He stared at me, said nothing, and snatched my passport.

He looked at the photo, flicked past a few pages, then stamped and returned it, before gesturing rather aggressively by pointing his right thumb over his left shoulder.

We never covered that one in our first-year gestures lesson, but I had a pretty fair idea of what it meant.

Milan's Malpensa Airport is quite some distance from the city itself, and for me, catching the train was the only viable means of getting into town.

I had booked and printed a ticket before I left the US, and I followed the signs to the station with my backpack aboard and suitcase in tow.

A train was standing next to the platform when I arrived, and it was less than a third full as I stowed my bags and sat down.

Within a few minutes, we were underway.

I was now officially in the country, and I sat quietly waiting for 'il Capitano del Treno' to inspect my ticket.

Booking and paying for my train tickets online had gone relatively smoothly. However, I was still a little nervous when il Capitano approached. After all, he was wearing an imposing red uniform, which was probably enough to intimidate just about anyone.

I presented him with my ticket, and he scanned the QR code printed at the top of the page. He nodded, said, "Bene," and I could relax for the remainder of the journey.

There wasn't much to see outside, and none of the other passengers paid any attention to me before we arrived at Milano Centrale station.

Everyone grabbed their bags and stepped off the train.

I followed suit, dragging my suitcase along the platform toward a massive concourse that presented a vast array of retail shops and advertising posters.

After negotiating a handful of staircases and following several signs marked, 'Uscita,' I was soon outside and within sight of a taxi stand that was doing a roaring trade.

There was a queue of people perhaps fifty strong, all carting suitcases and bags, one official-looking fellow coordinating the process, and another dodgy character who was touting for business with any number of private and unlicensed operators parked nearby.

As I joined the queue, he approached me, saying, "You need taxi?"

I thought to myself, "I am standing outside a busy railway station (at night) with two heavy bags. I am at the end of a queue (in what is clearly defined as a taxi stand) and it's raining."

"Gee, you don't miss much, do you?" I said.

"Special price," he responded.

"Piss off," I thought.

"No, thank you," I said.

Taxis were circling the stand and pulling up at regular intervals.

The only element that seemed to delay people's departure was when some of the smaller vehicles didn't have the capacity to stow the large amounts of luggage that accompanied some of the European aristocrats, Arab princes, and Hollywood celebrities at the head of the queue.

All the same, the process moved along quite smoothly, and I was eventually allocated to a small white vehicle that was driven by a very cheerful and friendly fellow.

I handed him a sheet of paper (upon which I had written the address of where I was staying) telling him, "Ho bisogno di andare a questo indirizzo." - I need to go to this address.

The address that I had given my driver read:

17 Via Villari

6 Bell Borelli

It soon transpired that the apartment building address was 17 Via Villari and that I should buzz or ring the doorbell for apartment number 6, which would be further defined with the name Borelli.

My driver negotiated the busy streets and persistent light rain while switching between the GPS app on his cell phone and the latest score updates from Inter Milan's European Champions League fixture, which was being played somewhere in Europe that same evening.

I don't know who Inter was playing, but it was late in the first half and they were leading 1-0.

A couple of weeks before I left, having already booked accommodation in Sulmona, Bari, and Rome, I trawled the Internet, expecting to find any number of hotel options where I could stay a couple of nights in Milan, before taking a train to the Abruzzo region east of Rome.

Well, that was an interesting exercise.

Having entered a couple of dates that confirmed a two-night stay, I was presented with at least fifteen pages of search results. Each page offered up more than a dozen hotels, with a handful of six-room dormitories (all with a shared bathroom) thrown in.

If not for the comparatively modest cost of the dormitories, anyone could have mistaken the prices listed for telephone numbers.

It simply wasn't realistic for me to travel any further than Milan so late in the day, and the idea had always been to stay close to the railway station.

But even the prospect of bumping into George Clooney 'down the shops,' wasn't enough to justify spending $800 a night in a hotel.

I seriously considered sleeping in the park, but the next day I found a spare room in an apartment that was defined as a 'rare find' on Airbnb and only available for one night.

I made a written application (in Italian) that was confirmed and accepted soon after.

Chapter 49

Milan

My taxi arrived at 17 Via Villari (with Inter Milan still leading 1-0) to see the name Borelli printed next to the doorbell button for Apartment 6.

I paid my driver, dragged my bags to the front door of the building, promised to support Inter Milan thereafter, and buzzed the doorbell.

"Buonasera. Secondo piano," was the response, as I collected my backpack and pushed against the door.

It was locked.

I buzzed again.

"Si," a voice said.

"Scusi," I replied, "missed the door."

This time I waited to hear the telltale sound of the front door's mechanical invitation, then pushed it open, dragging my suitcase inside before climbing a very narrow and steep concrete staircase.

Out of breath, by the time I reached the second floor, I was met by a woman who I suspect was in her early forties, with chaotic blonde hair and tattoos all over her wrists and hands.

She didn't welcome me so much as insist that I be quiet by raising her index finger to her lips and shushing me repeatedly.

She opened the door to her apartment, and as I struggled inside with my bags, she pointed toward the rear of the building and remarked, "There is an elevator."

"Really?" I responded, thinking, "Well, it's a bit late now."

She ushered me inside and immediately into a tiny bedroom that contained a single bed with a rickety metal frame. It had a mattress that was all of two inches thick and a tired old pillow that rested on an exhausted cotton sheet, beneath a polyester comforter that I reckon her dog slept on.

I didn't think I could possibly fit within the confines of the bed frame, and I asked if I could take the mattress off the bed and lay it on the floor.

My host didn't appear particularly impressed by the suggestion, and I quickly dispensed with the idea myself when I realized there simply wasn't room.

A small desk lamp was bolted to a narrow shelf that also housed a bottle of water.

That turned out to be breakfast.

Not that I have any immediate frame of reference you understand, but I reckon there are prison cells that are more luxuriously appointed.

I never saw the kitchen, but next door to my room was the bathroom.

It was narrow and cramped, with a shower reposing over a ceramic bathtub.

The bathroom walls were covered with an eclectic mix of pictures, mirrored signs, and shelves, all hanging amid an array of tiny potted plants and unrelated knick-knacks.

Finding my way around (in the middle of the night) would be a challenge.

I received no instruction as to where any light switches were located and swiftly ushered back into my room before being wished, "Buonanotte," as the door was closed.

I was exhausted all the same, and given I didn't harbor any great desire to get to know my host any better, I sat on the edge of the bed for a few minutes, lamenting the fact that this was the best I could do for $200, and grateful for the fact that I would be leaving early the following day.

But for the fact it was raining, I am not sure the park wouldn't have been a better option.

Under the circumstances, I slept reasonably well, making just one mid-night trip to the bathroom with the aid of a flashlight app on my cell phone.

I set an alarm for 7:30 am as my host had insisted that I vacate the premises by nine, and I wanted to leave time to shower, drink some water for breakfast, and locate the elevator.

The following day, I took the thin, coarse towel I had been allocated into the bathroom and drew back the shower curtain. This action proceeded to dismantle much of the rail from which the curtain itself was suspended, with one section breaking free from a cracked wall socket and falling onto the floor.

I picked up the offending section and re-attached both ends, before carefully maneuvering the curtain into place and tackling the hot water controls.

My shower was brief but adequate, as I was anxious to get in and out before anything else went wrong.

I returned to my room, stowed away the clothes I had worn the previous day, got dressed, and draped my now-damp towel over the bed frame.

I drank some water, gathered my belongings, and opened the door to my room to see my gracious host standing there, anxiously waiting to bid me farewell.

As I dragged my bags toward the door, she insisted (more than once) that if I should see or speak with any other resident of the building (particularly the landlord) I must tell them that she and I were old friends and that I was staying with her for just one night before continuing on my way.

Under no circumstances was I to even suggest that ours was any sort of commercial B&B (or B in my case) arrangement.

"Okay," I said, adding, "we are old friends."

"Si," she replied.

"I just have one question."

She rolled her eyes impatiently.

"What's that?"

"What is your name?" I replied.

"Oh, it's Martina," she said.

I went on to remark that if I were to engage in a conversation with a neighbor or her landlord, the likes of - 'Oh yes, the woman who lives at number six and I go way back. I have no idea what her name is, but we have been friends for years,' that they might conclude that she was operating a business much more nefarious in nature than anything one might find on Airbnb.

Martina then explained that there was a café nearby (where I could buy myself some breakfast) and that a nearby hospital was probably my best option when it came to finding a taxi that could take me back to the station.

She then opened the front door and ushered me outside, with a gesture that could only be realistically interpreted as -'Now get out!'

It certainly wasn't the most friendly, warm, and comfortable place to spend my first night in Italy, and in hindsight, perhaps $800 for a single night in a hotel might not have been such a bad option.

But on the other hand, how many hotels in Milan will have a life-size, free-standing, cardboard cut-out replica of Queen Elizabeth II (complete with jewels and crown) on display in the foyer?

Of course, when it's all said and done, these are the sort of things you need to bear in mind.

Chapter 50

Frecciarossa

I had planned on staying in Milan for two nights, but all that changed in the face of a $1,600 hotel bill, so I arranged to stay one night in Pescara.

Pescara was a destination en route to Sulmona, where I had confirmed a two-week stay in a studio apartment.

After consuming a cornetto and cappuccino at a local café (making good use of its covered outdoor seating area as it was still raining), I made tracks to the nearby hospital in anticipation of a plethora of taxis.

There wasn't much traffic outside the hospital at all, and there were no taxis in sight, as I stood patiently under my umbrella, secure in the knowledge that this probably was my best option.

My train was scheduled to leave Milano Centrale at 11:10 am, and with plenty of time to spare, I felt confident that a taxi would appear before long.

Sure enough, one did.

And not just any taxi, but quite possibly the only cab in all of Milan (if not Italy itself) that was driven by someone who wasn't up for a chat.

I stated that my destination was Milano Centrale, and apart from confirming the cost of the fare, that was about all we covered.

At the very least, I thought I might discover the outcome of the previous night's Champions League fixture, but it was not to be.

We arrived next to the same taxi stand I had briefly populated the night before, where I paid my fare, retrieved my bags, and walked into the station.

Mine was a Premium Business Class ticket on a Frecciarossa intercity service, which, though quite expensive, was not enough to gain access to the Freccia Lounge, where passengers could wait in relative comfort before their train was due to depart.

My lot was to wait on the platform with everyone else, scanning the departures board amid the chaos that ensues at Milano Centrale on a Thursday morning.

However, I did see a news headline that suggested the next round of Champions League fixtures would feature a clash between Milan's own two teams, Inter and AC, which I daresay is just about as big as it gets in this part of the world.

My train was indeed listed among the departures.

It appeared to be on time, unlike the Frecciarossa service on the platform directly in front of me, which, according to its departure information, was experiencing an eighty-minute delay.

Curiously, after what amounted to a delay of just fifty minutes, the train pulled out of the station, and as it journeyed beyond the end of the platform, the departures board was changed to confirm that the train had suffered a delay of thirty minutes less duration than it had previously indicated.

This may have come as something of a shock to those kicking back and sipping an espresso in the Freccia Lounge, but perhaps eighty minutes was always something of a worst-case scenario, and hopefully, those intending to travel on the train had already boarded.

In any case, the train itself was an express intercity service between Milan and Rome - so not likely to matter much to anyone.

Eventually, my train was allocated to platform 19.

I strolled across the concourse and walked along the platform to carriage number one.

As I did (even though I was inside a railway station housed beneath an enormous glass dome), rain started to fall. It was as if Milano Centrale was so huge that it had its own microclimate, but as I looked skywards, I could see that several glass panels in the roof above me were open.

I pondered the question, "Why bother having a roof at all if you are going to leave it open when it's raining?"

But there were more important things to be getting on with.

I stepped onto the train, where I had deliberately selected a seat next to a window and across from another two, with a table in between.

The idea was that I may get lucky and find myself seated opposite someone who might be interested to know where I was from, how long I was in Italy, fascinated to learn that I was writing a book, and above all, patient enough to tolerate my rudimentary Italian.

None of that happened.

I sat opposite two gentlemen, neither of whom seemed to find me the least bit interesting. One tapped away at a computer keyboard, while the other (who appeared to have banished his wife to a single seat across the aisle when one next to me and directly opposite him was vacant) inserted a pair of earphones and progressively worked his way through his cell phone's entire music library.

We did all get a bag of chips and a bottle of water though, so it wasn't a total loss.

Not long into the journey, I was feeling a little conspicuous wearing my polo shirt, shorts, and sneakers, as everyone else on the train appeared so well-dressed. Even the guy pushing the trash trolley along the aisle wore a suit.

The journey to Pescara would take just over four hours and three hours in I was starting to feel quite weary. The last thing I could afford to do was fall asleep and miss my stop, so I lost interest in the landscape that was racing past the windows and focused on simply staying awake.

Eventually, we passed through a few destinations that I could recall from my earlier research of the Marche and Abruzzo regions, which suggested Pescara wasn't far off.

I had demolished my chips long before but held off drinking the water, as I didn't particularly want to use a restroom on the train.

At last, Pescara was announced as the next station.

I dragged my backpack from an overhead rack (to hasten my exit), just in case the train only stopped briefly at the platform.

I needn't have worried, however, as the train fairly crawled into Pescara station, with any number of people queuing at its doors, anxious to stretch their legs on the platform.

I carried my backpack and dragged my suitcase, following the crowds to the concourse, where I spotted a couple of restrooms.

A man was seated outside and between the respective entrances. He was dressed top to toe in a bright green uniform, with the word 'Cleaner' writ large in black capital letters on his back.

A sign was attached to the wall behind him, indicating anyone could use the facilities for a fee of €1.00, and it wasn't a great leap to recognize that the cleaner would be collecting the money.

I could have haggled over the cost, assuring him that I would only be in there a few seconds and unlikely to make much of a mess.

Instead, I handed over a €5.00 note in exchange for a couple of coins and a printed receipt, upon which he had stamped both the time and date.

Soon after, I strolled to a nearby shop and bought a pizza slice that looked to comprise a tomato and salami base, topped with a generous portion of mozzarella.

I didn't expect much of any food that I could buy in a railway station, but heated up in a few minutes and washed down with the bottle of water I had been given on the train, it was absolutely delicious.

Given I would be returning to Pescara station in a couple of weeks (en route to Bari), I had half a mind to make a lunch booking.

I returned my empty tray with an enthusiastic, "Grazie mille, signora" and wandered outside in search of a taxi.

Chapter 51

Pescara

I had printed a map outlining the route to my hotel, but I was too tired to navigate and walk.

Happily, three or four taxis were lined up outside the station, and I spoke to the driver of the first one.

"Buonasera signore. Ho bisogno di andare all'albergo Fabri."- "Good evening, sir. I need to go to the Hotel Fabri."

He replied in impeccable English, "Yes, I know it, but the minimum fare is ten euros, and it's not a hotel, it's a BnB."

"Is it?" I said, staring at my booking confirmation, which gave every indication the accommodation was a hotel.

Ten euros and two minutes later, we arrived outside an apartment building around the corner from a shopping mall.

"There's a sign next to the door," my driver said, and sure enough, there was, with the word - Fabri, written in the same cursive type as it appeared on my receipt.

The door to the building was locked, and apart from the words - 'Secondo Piano,' printed beneath the Fabri logo on the exterior sign, there wasn't much to go on.

As luck would have it, someone was leaving the building, and I managed to sneak inside.

There was a narrow staircase in front of me, and (deploying my newly acquired knowledge of Italian architecture) I searched for an elevator at the rear of the building.

Sure enough, I found one, stepped inside, and traveled to the second floor.

I stepped out, and to my right, I could see a dark timber door with the same Fabri logo attached to it.

I knocked.

Nothing.

I knocked again.

Nothing.

In fact, I knocked about five times before I could hear the faint sound of footsteps climbing the stairs.

Hoping the footsteps might provide a solution, I waited.

Soon after, a young girl with pale, milky skin and the most glorious, curly brown hair reached the top of the stairs. She looked like an angel who had stepped out of a Botticelli painting, in order to execute some sort of divine intervention.

Her name was Chiara, she was from Sicily, and she was staying in one of the other rooms that comprised the Fabri BnB empire.

I explained my situation in Italian and (mostly) English. I didn't have a key, and I didn't know how to get a hold of one. I hadn't had any contact from anyone to explain how or what I was supposed to do, and short of the fact that I needed a key to exit the building, I would be spending the night on the beach.

"You need to ring this number," Chiara said, holding the screen of her cell phone for me to see.

"Could you?" I begged, as all my phone seemed able to do (at this point) was to receive (but not send) emails and present me with text messages from my US Telco, congratulating me on signing up for a $10.00 per day international call and Internet plan that didn't even work.

Chiara was kind enough to make the call, and a conversation followed.

I was optimistic at this point but still very anxious as I stood outside a locked door, behind which may lay the salvation I had paid for several weeks in advance.

Eventually, Chiara lowered the phone from her ear, and while her other party was still on the line, she uttered my favorite word in the Italian language.

"Allora."

Allora is a word our substitute teacher Annika used before introducing a new subject or element during class. An Italian dictionary might define it as meaning 'so,' but it has a much broader definition than that. It can also mean, 'right then, or okay,' as might be expressed to introduce a new direction in a conversation or a solution to a problem.

In this case, I took it to mean, "It's okay Michael, don't panic. The matter is in hand, and we will soon have you inside. Everything will be fine. You won't be trapped inside the building, and you won't be sleeping under the stairs or on the beach."

That's a pretty elaborate definition for a word of three syllables.

As if by magic, Chiara produced a set of keys out of thin air, one of which would unlock the main door and a key card that would allow me to access my room.

While still carrying on her telephone conversation, she ushered me into my room, opened the door to the bathroom, and pointed to some towels sitting on a chair.

When I inquired "What about breakfast?" she put her hand on an espresso machine and lifted one of two coffee pods from a small basket.

It was a step up from a bottle of water at least.

Eventually, she hung up the phone, which allowed me to thank her for saving the day.

"Tomorrow," I said, "perhaps I can buy you a coffee?"

She pointed at the espresso machine.

"No," I said, to say thank you. I don't know what I would have done if it wasn't for you."

I invited her to sit down, and we chatted for a few minutes, which allowed me to congratulate and encourage her worthwhile command of English.

She left the keys on a bench (at the foot of the bed) and explained that I needed to insert the key card in its socket (just inside the door) to turn the lights on and off.

I didn't dare leave the room (let alone the building) and settled in for an early night, before catching a train to Sulmona the next day.

As I lay in bed, it struck me that I didn't have the faintest idea what to do with the keys or key card the following day, which in the grand scheme of things was hardly a big deal, but it did prey on my mind all the same.

I was all of two days/nights into a two-month itinerary, and to date, things hadn't gone quite as well as I had hoped, but at least I wasn't curled up under the stairs or sleeping on the beach.

The following day, I fired up the espresso machine, not realizing the capsule that it already contained had been 'spent.'

After suffering through a tiny cup of coffee-flavored hot water, I added a new capsule, one that was able to generate something with a kick to it.

I then wrote a note for Chiara and slipped it under her door.

I said I wanted to thank her again for helping me, that she will always be my friend, and should our paths ever cross again (via the medium of my email address), I would do all I could to help her in any circumstance.

I also said that I would leave the keys and card in my room (with the door unlocked) and that if she didn't mind returning them to wherever she managed to conjure them from in the first place, I would be very grateful.

Having packed my things, I strode confidently to the elevator and descended to the ground floor, completely forgetting that I needed one of the keys that Chiara had given me to unlock the front door of the building.

I returned to my room, grabbed the keys, and journeyed downstairs again. This time, I unlocked the front door, propping it open with my suitcase, before racing back upstairs, leaving the keys on a bench and the door to my room ajar.

I then returned to the ground floor, to see my suitcase reposing in a manner whereby the front door was still open. I stepped outside (letting the door slam shut behind me) and made tracks to a café two doors up.

It really is remarkable what a cappuccino and a pistachio cornetto can do to lift your mood.

Having addressed my appetite and coffee craving, I started making my way to the station, remembering that we had passed a TIM retail outlet in my ten-euro taxi ride the previous day.

I am still not sure what TIM stands for, but my money is on Telecom Italia Mobile.

In any case, TIM seems to sponsor just about anything that moves in Italy (and a few things that don't), so I entrusted them with the task of inserting a new SIM card into my cell phone, which would hopefully give me access to emails, text messages, the Internet, and the occasional GPS endeavor.

€25.00 would do just that for a month, and another €20.00 would extend that contract for a further four weeks.

I signed a four-page agreement (that anyone would need a magnifying glass to read) three times, and I could only hope that when I returned to New York, I wouldn't discover that the TIM corporation already owned my apartment, car, and other worldly possessions.

In any case, I had a new (albeit temporary) cell phone number.

Now all I had to do was work out how to switch off the $10.00 per day international call and Internet plan, that I was being constantly congratulated for unknowingly signing up to in the first place.

Chapter 52

Sulmona

I was concerned that the train from Pescara might be more crowded, and at the very least, less comfortable than the Frecciarossa intercity service I had taken from Milan. The Pescara to Sulmona route was a regional service by comparison and unlikely to boast the sort of sleek, modern, rolling stock that proudly featured at the top of the page on the Trenitalia website.

Seats were unreserved, and there was no class distinction to select from. The train's entire capacity was rated Second Class, and it was simply a matter of showing up and making the best of it.

My concerns were entirely unfounded, however, as I boarded a train that was every bit as modern and comfortable as the service I had taken from Milan.

Only a handful of people were seated in my carriage, and 'la Capitana del Treno' (who checked my ticket) was very friendly and courteous.

All in all, it's a shame the trip lasted just over an hour.

The last portion of my journey to Pescara followed the coast, where I was treated to views of the Adriatic and its sandy beaches. Within thirty minutes of traveling to Sulmona, I was reveling in the sight of snow-capped mountains disappearing into the clouds.

The landscape's transformation was as spectacular as it was sudden.

Ancient stone buildings sat atop hills in the shadow of those same mountains, while goats and sheep grazed on low-lying pastures.

Sheer cliff faces were smothered in a thick blanket of trees, celebrating countless shades of green, as our train carved a route through the valley below.

We arrived on time at Sulmona station and having stepped off the train, I spoke to a fellow at the ticket office, asking where I could catch the bus.

My train booking had included the additional option of taking a bus to Sulmona Centro.

It was a service that I hoped would deliver me close enough to my lodgings to complete the remainder of the journey on foot.

The fellow I spoke with cheerfully directed me outside, where I could fully appreciate the majesty of the mountains.

I returned a few seconds later, to be ushered outside again and to the right of the station building.

"Si certo," I replied, adding, "Le montagne sono magnifiche!" - The mountains are magnificent.

He nodded and smiled, conveying a polite indifference that suggested he had spent most of his life in the company of such a majestic natural wonder.

Which, to be fair, he almost certainly had.

The bus arrived a few minutes later. Four or five of us got on board, and we journeyed in and around the outskirts of Sulmona, passing a handful of churches and several cafés before our journey ended outside a hospital, where the pavement was fractured, uneven, and very much suitcase-wheel unfriendly.

It didn't look all that 'centro' to me, and as I stepped off the bus, I thanked the driver, asking him, "Dove posso comprare una mappa di Sulmona?" - "Where can I buy a map of Sulmona?" He presented me with a very detailed reply, of which I understood not a single word, other than the fact that at one stage, he had pointed straight ahead.

"Grazie signore," I said.

I walked along the pavement and a few minutes later spotted a small shop on the other side of the road that was defined as a 'tabaccheria,' and perhaps somewhere where I could buy a map.

I crossed the road, entered the shop, and said, "Scusi signore, ma ho bisogno di comprare una mappa di Sulmona."

The shopkeeper walked to the back of his store, rummaged through a few items on a shelf, and returned, handing me a folded map.

"Grazie signore," I said, adding, "Quanto costa?" - How much does it cost?

He dismissed my question in a manner that indicated, "Don't worry about it."

"È gratuita?" - It's free? I asked.

"Si," he replied.

"Grazie mille," I said, deciding right then and there, 'I like Sulmona."

After all, here you just have to show up, and someone will give you a map of the town for free. In Pescara, they charge you €1.00 to use the restroom.

I stood outside the shop for a moment, where an elderly woman (walking with the aid of a stick) addressed me as, "Signore," while clearly asking me to help her step up from the pavement and into the store.

She took hold of my arm and lifted herself up, patting the back of my hand repeatedly while saying, "Grazie. Grazie."

I thought her descent onto a treacherous section of pavement would prove even more dangerous, so I waited for her to leave.

However, she was engaged in a long and detailed conversation with the shopkeeper, so I shuffled down the street with my suitcase in tow.

Before long, I reached a small park, where I sat opposite a fountain and tried to make sense of my new map, together with the address of where I was staying.

Just then, I received a message from my BnB host.

I replied, telling him that I was now in Sulmona, but needed to figure out exactly where.

Technology was winning the day, so rather than wrestle with a map of many folds, I used my cell phone's GPS function, plugged in some earphones, and did what it told me for the next fifteen minutes.

I walked along some beautiful cobbled streets and past some fascinating buildings and statues, including one of a famous ancient Roman poet named Ovid, who was born in Sulmo, as Sulmona was known in 43 BC.

Ovid was quite a celebrity in his day until he did something to upset Emperor Augustus, who chose to banish him to a town on the shores of the Black Sea in what today is Romania.

No one seems to know exactly what Ovid did or said to receive what (at the time) was considered a very cruel and ruthless punishment, while Ovid's own recollection of the incident is particularly cryptic.

'A poem and a mistake,' he is quoted as saying, as to why he lived out his declining years in Eastern Europe.

Whether or not the poem itself was a mistake, or the poem led to a mistake, or perhaps the two elements were effectively unrelated but together resulted in his demise, no one seemed to know.

However, he is remembered and honored with a rather imposing statue in Sulmona's Piazza Settembre, so I think it's fair to say the locals still rate him.

Eventually, I spotted a Tourist Information Center (housed in a very grand old building) just as I was instructed to turn right, then left into a very narrow Via Paolina.

Standing outside number 17 (a sixteenth-century, three-story stone building) was my host Paolo, who was cradling his young daughter in his arms.

She reluctantly let go of his neck, and we shook hands before he opened the door to the building and introduced me to apartment number 4, which would be my home for the next two weeks.

The property was defined as a studio, which is a flash word for a one-room apartment with a tiny kitchen and a separate bathroom.

Importantly though, it was clean, comfortable, and perfectly adequate.

It housed a small sofa and a double bed. Towels, cooking utensils, bowls, plates, and cutlery were provided. There was a small table (with two chairs) underneath a television and three wall-mounted radiators, two in the bedroom/lounge/kitchen and one in the bathroom. The radiators were set to a timer (morning and evening) and a reverse-cycle air-conditioning unit was mounted above the door.

It wasn't spacious, and it wasn't luxurious, but it was hard to fault. Particularly given Paolo had included breakfast vouchers (that I could redeem each day of my stay) with a café just around the corner.

He handed over a set of keys, assured me that I could contact him anytime, and wished me a pleasant stay.

There is a woman in Milan (renting a spare room) who could learn a lot from Paolo.

At last, I felt I could relax and that I was at home.

The apartment had three windows. One looked out onto Via Paolina and the other two onto a small courtyard. Each window featured timber shutters and curtains that (when closed and locked) rendered the apartment devoid of natural light at any time of the day or night.

I unpacked my things, storing them in a set of drawers and a closet. I then charged my cell phone and made tracks to a small supermarket I had passed on the way.

Chapter 53

Caffè Ovidio

My first order of business, every morning, was to visit Caffè Ovidio and redeem my la colazione voucher.

Each voucher entitled me to an espresso, cappuccino, or a cup of tea, together with 'un cornetto' or an equivalent (invariably sweet) pastry.

This is how I came to learn that the word for custard donut (in Sulmona, at least) is bomba.

The café was owned by a gregarious, colorful fellow and staffed by two much younger employees, possibly offspring.

We adopted a curious arrangement, whereby I would do my best each day to speak to them in Italian, and they would invariably respond to me in English.

It was like playing a round of, 'Anything you can do, I can do better.'

I would always order a cappuccino and sit at the rear of the café, where I could be a fly on the wall, eavesdropping on various conversations that (try as I may) I could never make head nor tail of.

For the most part, café patrons would fit into one of two categories:

1. Those who stood at the bar, sipping an espresso, often drinking it in less time than it took to make.

2. Those who sat at tables, sipping an espresso, often drinking it in less time than it took to make.

I, by comparison, would sit quietly, sipping my cappuccino and consuming my pastry before returning my empty cup to the bar and ordering another coffee.

I soon gathered the impression that this was a rather strange thing to do.

Ordering a second cup of coffee was met with a degree of concern and bemusement before I justified my desire by saying, "Questo è il migliore cappuccino in Abruzzo."

Given that I had been in the entire region less than three days, I really wasn't in a position to render anyone's cappuccino as the best in Abruzzo, but I daresay the sentiment was appreciated.

I would pay for my second cappuccino each morning and generally make my way up il Corso Ovidio, which had a glorious cobblestone surface and was part pedestrian mall, part motorway.

That might seem an awkward and even dangerous combination, but I was unfailingly impressed with motorists' patience when driving amongst and alongside pedestrians in Sulmona. I never saw or heard a driver sound a car horn, or call out to anyone wandering or standing in their way.

Not even when some fool stood smack bang in the middle of the road taking a photograph, although I did try not to make a habit of that.

Every second shop in the street looked to be selling small packets of confetti, with proud retailers standing outside their stores, presenting their colorful displays and creations to any number of people who (for the most part) simply filed past.

I began to wonder just how viable some of these businesses were, and I was genuinely concerned for some, if for no other reason than they created such a charming atmosphere.

Mind you, the same could be said of Sulmona's cafés.

I have never known a city, town, village, or neighborhood with such an abundance of them. Forget the old adage, there's one on every corner. In Sulmona, there is likely to be one next door.

Weekends in il Corso Ovidio were busier than weekdays, and mornings, much busier than afternoons. In the evening, however, the whole place would erupt with the phenomenon of 'La Passeggiata.'

Hundreds of people would stroll up and down il corso, all well-dressed and often walking arm-in-arm. It was the only way to see and be seen in Sulmona, and the entire mood amongst great crowds of people was invariably cheerful, friendly, and positively celebratory.

La Passeggiata is a fascinating event to witness, as it has no specific structure or process. It's just something that people do, and while a lot of those involved may find their way to some of the town's many ristoranti, trattorie, and pizzerie afterward, it is less of a pre-dinner appetizer and more of a cultural and community tradition.

Chapter 54

Tailspin

As I fumbled with my cell phone in the rear of the café one morning, it became clear that I could receive emails and WhatsApp messages (thanks to my new SIM card), but any emails I tried to send in reply were bounced back as invalid.

Dopo il mio secondo cappuccino, I wandered up il corso and called into a retail store that (judging by the number of corporate logos displayed on its window) represented just about every Internet and cell phone network provider in the country, TIM included.

As I entered the shop, I could see two employees and one customer, all of whom would cheerfully join forces to resolve my email issue.

None of them spoke any English, but I was able to explain my problem with a mixture of schoolboy Italian and elaborate gestures, whereby I communicated the phrase, "Email a me è bene, ma quando invio - niente," after which I further confessed, "Sono confuso."

One of the two employees took hold of my phone and dug into its email accounts and settings. He composed a couple of emails to his colleague, and once one of them actually got through, he presented me with a solution that (in hindsight) was as obvious as it was effective.

"Solo Gmail," he said, "Non gli altri." - Not the others.

In short, I should only and always use my Gmail account when sending, and not any other accounts that were (no doubt) connected to a local US email server.

Pretty obvious when you think about it.

The customer then took hold of my phone and showed me a message that one of the two employees had sent to his colleague.

It simply read, "Ciao."

"No," I responded, insisting, "Ciao e grazie!" which everyone seemed to get a great kick out of. Not least of all, me.

It was a Wednesday this day and one of two days each week when a market was set up in the Piazza Garibaldi.

I had passed the piazza when first walking to my apartment in Via Paolina. It covered at least five acres, with a spectacular fountain at its center, and I felt sure its market would present a host of stalls and a hive of activity to wander amongst and photograph.

However, I made a fateful detour before I even got there.

A tabaccheria, located on a street corner, displayed any number of postcards outside its front door, and I decided (then and there) that this was an opportunity to fulfill my entire correspondence obligations in one fell swoop.

I collected ten cards from a rack and bought ten stamps from the shopkeeper, having been assured that the stamps would prove a sufficient investment for all ten cards to arrive safely in the USA and Australia, respectively.

The total came to €28.00, and given the shopkeeper wanted to be paid in cash, I handed over my last €20.00 note and paid the balance with my pre-paid travel debit card.

I then collected the postcards and stamps in a small paper bag, put them in my backpack and walked up the street toward the piazza.

When I reached the top of the steps leading down to the piazza, I could see a market crammed with all manner of stalls, selling everything from clothing and shoes to fruit and vegetables.

That's when I first felt for the rigid plastic of my debit card, housed inside my elaborate and expensive, scan-proof money belt.

All I could feel was fabric.

I clenched various portions in my fist, desperately searching and hoping to feel my card housed safely inside.

I felt nothing. Not even a bank note or a coin.

I stretched the waistband out so I could see the whole thing. I unzipped each of its three pouches and turned the entire contraption inside out. I checked every pocket in my shirt and trousers (more than once), emptied my backpack, and searched inside the paper bag that housed my postcards.

There was no brand new and expensively laden debit card to be seen or felt anywhere, and the supposedly impregnable fortress that was my money belt had proven an epic fail at its first opportunity.

I could feel my face burning with a blend of anxiety and fear before I collected my thoughts and returned to the same tabaccheria, where I had quite possibly just bought the world's most expensive postcards.

I spoke to the shopkeeper and explained, "Signore, ho perso la mia carta di credito."

Strictly speaking, it wasn't a credit card, and mine may not have been the most perfect Italian, but at this point, I didn't particularly care, and given the circumstances, I figured close enough would do.

If nothing else, the look of sheer panic on my face would have filled in any gaps.

"Hai lo scontrino?" he asked.

I had never come across the word for receipt before, but I figured, 'scontrino' was it.

Oddly enough, I did have lo scontrino, which the shopkeeper then used to access the store's overhead CCTV footage and replay our entire transaction on his cell phone.

This clearly demonstrated two things:

    1. The shopkeeper most definitely returned my card.

    2. I really need to lose some weight.

While slipping my card back inside its pouch, I had, apparently, missed my money belt entirely, and perhaps tucked it inside the waistband, before losing it in the street.

I asked anyone and everyone in the shop if they had seen it.

No one had.

The shopkeeper then suggested, "Devi parlare con la polizia," before he ushered me out of his store and demonstrated that there was a police station not thirty yards away, in the same narrow laneway that cornered his own business.

I didn't expect anything to come of it, and to be honest, I didn't really expect any police officer to particularly care.

Even so, I wandered up there, opened the door, and walked inside.

Three uniformed officers were floating around the front desk.

They were soon joined by two others, no doubt curious to know what all the commotion was about, and just who it was who was speaking such appalling Italian.

None of them spoke any English, and I didn't know who to address specifically, so I worked my way around the room, looking at each of them in turn, saying, "Io sono australiano, e ho perso la mia carta di credito nella strada. È il mio solo soldi."

Again, far from perfect, but I daresay my disheveled, panicked expression got the message across.

All of the officers remained completely calm and quiet before one of them spoke, asking me, "Di che colore è?"

I could remember working with that very same question in our first year of classes when Annika filled in for la professoressa, holding various articles of clothing and colored pencils aloft in class.

"Nero," I said, and the officer left the room.

I was just about to light up the afterburners and go into a full-on tailspin when he returned a few seconds later with a black travel debit card that someone had handed in a few minutes earlier.

It looked a lot like mine, but even I had to check the signature on the back to be sure.

I gestured to him as if to say, "Do you want me to sign something for you to check and prove that this is mine?"

The officer waved away my suggestion.

I then asked him, "Do you know the person's name?"

He just shrugged his shoulders.

Shaking his hand vigorously, I said, "Grazie, grazie mille," repeating the process with each of his four colleagues (all of whom probably had nothing to do with the entire episode) before I returned to the tabaccheria, recalled the whole adventure, and did my best to congratulate the shopkeeper for having the good sense to locate his business in the vicinity of a police station.

I then did what any mature and responsible individual would do in the circumstances.

I celebrated with an enormous chocolate and pistachio gelato.

The diet can start tomorrow.

Chapter 55

Musical Pagans

One of the many delightful and unique quirks of Sulmona is that every day (shortly after 8:00 am) some joker will play, 'Name That Tune' on a set of church bells somewhere in the town.

At eight o'clock every morning, a sequence of bells will ring out. Curiously, eleven times.

This sequence will be followed a minute or so later by a chorus (perhaps twenty seconds or so) from a modern-day pop song, played with remarkable precision on any number of church bells.

The tunes are almost always recognizable, if not immediately identifiable, and the whole process can be as frustrating as it is entertaining.

I soon adopted a habit of sitting at a table and opening one of the window shutters (regardless of the weather) to hear each day's tune more clearly.

It didn't necessarily make it any easier to identify, but it made the whole process even more fun and gave me a fighting chance.

All in all, I had a crack at a dozen tunes. I recognized most and identified two.

After breakfast, I strolled along il corso to the post office, entrusted my postcards to the Italian postal service, and returned via La Piazza Garibaldi.

Preparations were underway for an event in the piazza.

Four huge piles of branches, sticks, and thatch surrounded the fountain at its center, and a stage was being constructed nearby.

I love a good bonfire, and the prospect of four was particularly exciting.

I hovered for a few minutes, close to a team of people (who were clearly in charge), and when a couple broke ranks for a moment, I asked what time the event was scheduled to start.

I returned that evening at eight o'clock, and it was 8:30 pm before anything happened.

A fellow stepped up on stage and introduced himself (with the aid of a microphone) to what was quite a large crowd.

Just so we could be sure what his role was, he was wearing a bright red jacket with the word, Speaker emblazoned on the back.

He spoke for far too long before introducing another fellow, who was wearing a dark suit, and who talked for even longer.

He might have been the mayor. Not that anyone seemed to care.

Eventually, he handed the microphone back to the speaker, who introduced a colorful and energetic musical performance by a group of ten or so people dressed in costumes that were fashioned in leather and fur, evoking something of the region's hunter-gatherer and pagan history.

They paraded in front of the stage, playing large drums and instruments (that resembled bagpipes) to the delight and fascination of the many children present, to say nothing of the odd tourist.

I was very impressed by one fellow in particular. He had a bass drum strapped to his chest, and his face was crudely adorned with thick stripes of a dark blue pigment. He marched around with passion and purpose from start to finish, engaging the audience as best he could throughout.

I had spotted him earlier (before the performance), relaxing with his colleagues. He was leaning against a pickup truck and decanting a bottle of mineral water into a cow horn.

Full marks for engagement and presentation, I say.

The performance lasted for about ten minutes, and it immediately preceded the lighting of the bonfires.

A couple of official-looking people shoved some long, fiery poles (which looked like giant matchsticks) under the base of the stacks, as each one was subsequently set ablaze.

Up to that point, hundreds of people had gathered close by. Many were pressed against a temporary security fence surrounding the fire stacks and fountain.

All of us retreated at least ten feet once the fires took hold.

The next day, the piazza had been cleaned up, with the stage and fencing stacked away.

The bonfires had been set atop a thick blanket of sand, and I daresay those in charge knew what they were doing when it came time to restore everything to its original condition.

Just as well, as it was soon market day again.

The Sulmona market is a significant local event that conveys a colorful and vibrant representation of the town.

I had missed the process of everyone bringing everything in and setting up, but I am willing to bet it was chaotic.

For one thing, there looked to be only one vehicle access point.

A couple of food trucks (selling pork rolls and cooked chickens at the far end of the piazza) would have had to arrive very early or traverse a precarious path to their designated site.

However it came about, it all worked, as everyone had their own patch, and for the most part, it all made sense.

Fruit, vegetable, egg, and garlic vendors were located on one side of the piazza, as were a couple of vans selling various types of cheese and prosciutto.

Clothes and shoes bordered the far side of the piazza and its top end, while stalls arranged back to back (on either side of a general corridor section) ranged from hats, bags, and cooking utensils to underwear, stockings, and an assortment of hardware.

The busiest stalls (without a doubt) sold clothing, with one displaying a sign that boasted:

Merce Fresca. Prezzi Caldi!   Fresh Goods. Hot Prices!

I never saw how the clothing stalls looked before the market opened, but given people were constantly folding and rearranging the stock (to present it in its best possible light), things probably started out looking pretty neat and tidy.

The problem with the whole folding and stacking strategy was that once two or three women descended upon a stall, they would pick up a garment, hold it up to the light, turn it around, and most often toss it aside, repeating the process over and over, so that in less than a minute, the entire display became a tortured and unholy mess.

To their great credit, however, the market minions soldiered on, gathering, folding, and stacking clothes as quickly and neatly as possible.

It was certainly an interesting and often quite comical spectacle.

Why they even bothered, I honestly can't say.

Having completed a few laps of the market and seen all there was to see, I decided to climb a set of broad, stone steps leading up to il corso.

The steps had been worn smooth by centuries of foot traffic, and (as a consequence) they were very slippery.

At least that's the excuse I am offering, to explain the clumsy and spectacular fall that I executed when I was about a third of the way up.

My sneakered left foot slipped backward from one of the steps, just as I felt my ample weight lurch immediately forward.

I did all I could to recover my balance, before colliding with a medieval stone construct (hitting myself in the head with a cooked chicken in the process) and rolling awkwardly onto the surface of the piazza.

People rushed from everywhere to help and to ask if I was okay.

There was practically a queue.

As painful and embarrassing as it was, I did my best to brush the whole thing off (as if I hadn't felt a thing) before politely declining an offer of help from one woman in particular, who suggested that she and her friend could help me climb the steps by holding on to one of my arms each.

It was very kind of her, but still rather galling, given both she and her friend were much older than me.

I thanked everyone involved very much for their concern and declared that I would instead walk across to the far side of the piazza.

That way, I could stroll up the modest gradient of a long cobblestone ramp, while doing my best to act as if nothing had ever happened.

Chapter 56

Shit Scared

Everyone said you must visit Scanno, a unique and beautiful village frozen in time and nestling at the top of the Apennine Mountains.
Deborah from my Italian class had said it, my Italy travel guide mentioned it, and even the delightful and patient Francesca from Sulmona's Tourist Information Center suggested it.

I even discussed it with Paolo, my B&B host. He thought it was a good idea too, but recommended hiring a car rather than taking a bus.

Paolo was on to something.

Apparently, there are two roads one can take when traveling from Sulmona to Scanno.

One is relatively benign. It is picturesque (even spectacular) and entirely suitable for large vehicles (like buses) carrying several passengers.

Then there's the road we took.

A narrow, treacherous strip of asphalt that winds its way through a series of sheer cliff faces and bottomless vertical drops, that, to be fair, does unveil some extraordinary scenery if you are not too terrified to enjoy it.

I bought a return ticket at the tourist office and boarded a bus, where it stopped under il Ponte Capograssi.

I even managed to secure a seat at the front of the vehicle, just behind the driver's right shoulder, looking over the passenger stairwell and past a ticket validation machine.

This strategy allowed me to enjoy a panoramic view of the journey presented through a large, flat, and clear windshield.

In hindsight, this was a mistake.

We soon left Sulmona and journeyed to the outskirts of Introdacqua, before collecting a couple of passengers in the village of Bugnara.

By this stage, I think we had seven or eight brave souls on board.

Our ascent into the mountains soon followed, with the terrain getting steeper and the road narrower.

At one point, our driver had to slam on the brakes as we all but wedged ourselves against a van traveling in the other direction that had just swept around an entirely blind corner.

As we did, I glanced to my right to see that our rear-view mirror was buried in some tangled vegetation.

Below a mass of vines and leaves was a photograph of a young man, a bunch of flowers, and a printed message that was no doubt paying tribute to a recent road accident victim.

Happily, the van managed to sneak past, and we were soon on our way again.

The scenery was astonishing, with chiseled cliff faces to one side and dense forests the other before we reached one section where the road wound its way around a sheer precipice to the left while offering an immediate vertical drop and certain death to the right.

All that stood between us and a spiraling descent into the valley below was a two-foot-high stone wall that a sixty-four-seat passenger bus could crash through (with all the ease of a weightlifter crushing an empty aluminum can) should the slightest error of judgment ensue.

At least the driver could hug the inside of the road and stay close to the rock face, but every time we negotiated a sweeping bend, the front wheels of the bus would turn just short of the wall, which momentarily left my entire section floating over the cliff's edge.

This stretch of road continued for a couple of miles, and it took perhaps five or six minutes to traverse.

It felt like an hour.

Especially given our driver chose this particular section of road and this specific moment in time to answer his phone!

And not via some hands-free speaker setup, mind you.

Oh no, not at all. He spent the entire time steering his bus around the world's most dangerous stretch of highway, holding his cell phone in his left hand (pressed against his ear) and the steering wheel (most of the time) in his right.

He did, of course, have to let go of it any number of times to change gears.

I had no idea what he was talking about or who he was speaking to, and I didn't dare interrupt. I just wrapped my fists around a yellow metal railing (that sat above the stairwell) and did all I could to rip it out of the floor.

Eventually, our driver hung up his phone just as we reached a less frightening stretch of road, which presented some beautiful views of Lago di Scanno.

Local legend suggests that the lake was formed after a violent feud between a witch and a sorcerer. The sorcerer won the day, and the lake was formed where and when the witch finally met her end.

Soon after, we arrived in Scanno, and the bus pulled up alongside a small triangular piazza.

I thanked our driver and stepped off (tackling one step at a time) before bracing myself against a wall and slowly shuffling across the street, where I sat on a timber bench for the next five minutes or so.

My legs felt like jelly and my shirt was stuck to my back, but given that Scanno had been around for hundreds of years, I felt sure it wouldn't mind if I didn't explore its tangle of laneways and sturdy gray-stone houses for a few minutes yet.

The town's landscape mirrored its surroundings, rising sharply in parts with several steep, narrow stairwells and alleys.

You would soon get fit if you lived here.

As I walked in and around the town, I noticed that much like Sulmona, Scanno boasts several drinking fountains that are located in the street, where traumatized tourists can quench their thirst and settle their nerves with the cleanest, crispest, and coldest natural spring water that I for one have ever tasted.

The water was so pure and clear that I felt I could break a stream of it off in my hands and snap it in two.

At one point, I walked past a sign that reminded people to be on the lookout for bears.

The area also boasts a population of wolves, but perhaps they have their own sign.

In any case, no one should ever approach a bear. Never get out of your car if you see a bear, and don't ask a bear to get out of the way. Don't even think of sharing a packed lunch with one, and never make it easy for bears to dine out on any food scraps you might leave lying around, lest they treat such things as an appetizer and fancy you as a main course.

After wandering around for more than an hour and getting hopelessly lost, I stumbled upon the same small piazza where my expedition had begun, from where I could see the same bus that had brought us here parked across the road.

The bus would return to Sulmona, and it was scheduled to leave in twenty minutes, so rather than risk getting lost again in the narrow streets of Scanno, I chose to sit in the sun, relax, and contemplate my fate.

Many of the passengers who had traveled from Sulmona earlier in the day made the same return journey, and I thought it would be downright cowardly of me to sit anywhere else.

So once again, I secured a position at the front of the vehicle, hoping and praying that the battery on our driver's cell phone was flat.

We took the same route on the return leg, passing the wonderful Lago di Scanno and traversing the same narrow, winding stretch of road that had me seriously contemplating my own mortality a few hours before.

It was still pretty hair-raising, but given I had survived the experience the first time around and this time, the driver's wife didn't feel the need to give him a call, I managed to get through it okay, while still giving that metal railing a good working over.

If you should ever catch a bus from Sulmona, grab hold of the yellow metal handrail at the top of the stairwell as you get on board.

If it's a bit loose, that was me.

Chapter 57

Museo Civico

I had breakfast at Caffè Ovidio, where I witnessed three men (two quite elderly and another relatively young) having an intense and animated discussion about God knows what.

I don't know if it was politics, the environment, or whether Juventus should dispense with its latest 4-4-2 combination, but one of the older ones was hammering home a point by gesturing extravagantly, and practically stabbing his friend in the face with a cornetto.

It's probably just as well he could take a few bites while one of the other two was speaking. Otherwise, someone might have lost an eye in the process.

Mind you, a mouthful of pastry was clearly no impediment when he wanted to express an opinion.

The weather forecast was bleak, so I decided to visit Sulmona's Museo Civico, which was located next door to the Tourist Information Center in the Annunziata Church Complex, a building that had once housed the convent of Santa Chiara.

Note to self, Chiara of Pescara wasn't an angel but a saint.

I paid €8.00 for a 'Combined Ticket' that said seven, and it wasn't until I studied an accompanying brochure (the next day) that I realized I had been locked out of an entire section.

Specific exhibits were presented in separate rooms that surrounded a stone-paved courtyard, some upstairs and some down, with signs pointing up, down, and across, respectively.

I appeared to be the museum's only patron that day and (following a sign) crossed a section of the courtyard before climbing a steep, slippery stone staircase, only to be met by a locked door.

Returning to the courtyard, while rehearsing the phrase 'Scusi, signore, ma la porta è chiusa,' I could see the ticket seller (who spoke no English) was talking on the phone, so I reconfigured my strategy and found another exhibit that presented various Bronze Age tools, weapons, and implements.

The tools had been unearthed in the local area and possibly fashioned by ancestors of the Musical Pagans who had performed at the Piazza Garibaldi bonfire celebration.

I climbed another staircase only to be met by another locked door before I discovered a ground-floor Roman section that was worth every bit of the €8.00 entry fee.

The Domus di Arianna was the remains of an ancient Roman villa, discovered in 1991 and dating from the first century BC.

A metal walkway had been installed so that people like me could wander just above its remains and see the various rooms that once comprised the house.

Five rooms surrounded a small patio that probably housed a tank for collecting rainwater.

Some of the internal walls had been lost, although several portions were still visible, while wall coverings that represented various myths and legends had been partially restored.

Apparently, the wall coverings portrayed the sacred union of Dionysus and Ariadne, together with the quarrel between Eros and Pan - according to the museum's brochure anyway.

A section of clear Plexiglas in the walkway rests above a portion of mosaic flooring (that, but for the presence of my left foot, made for a striking photograph) in what is generally regarded as a very well-appointed dwelling for its time.

The first three rooms of the house were most likely reception rooms, while two others at the back had more coarse flooring and are thought to have served a more practical purpose.

One of these rooms still retains some of its dome-shaped roof. My money is on kitchen, with stones of various shapes all held together with a mortar that has lasted for more than two thousand years.

It is a fascinating exhibit, complemented by other Roman artifacts, ranging from stone tablets featuring numerous Latin inscriptions to more everyday objects such as bottles, jugs, eating utensils, and coins.

Another section of the museum housed several free-standing mannequins, all dressed in the traditional costumes that women wore in different parts of the Abruzzo region during the nineteenth century.

Most people were sheep farmers back then (in Abruzzo, anyway) and women's clothing changed little over the years.

By contrast, men's attire varied more, given they often moved about in search of work and had a wider sphere of cultural influence to draw upon.

The women's costumes were invariably colorful, intricate, and ornate. They consisted of long dresses that covered white cotton blouses with delicate headscarves.

Just what you need when you spend all day working in the fields.

There was one striking male mannequin on display as well. He was presented in hunting attire and surrounded by his various weapons.

He was dressed in a black cape with a dark fur collar, fastened by a brass neck chain, and wearing a broad-brimmed, black felt hat.

He looked like he could easily blend into a dense forest background and that he was not someone to be trifled with.

Not if you were a bear or a wolf anyway.

Chapter 58

Pacentro

It was my last full day in Sulmona, and the weather had improved. It was a sunny 23 degrees, and I decided to catch a bus to the nearby village of Pacentro.

Pacentro is an Italian word meaning, 'a tiny community of houses and one imposing castle that nestles in the side of a mountain.'

A bus was due to call past my stop at 10:25 am, and I was impressed (at first) when one did, only to find its driver answer, "No, arriva," when I asked him, "Andiamo a Pacentro?"

The word 'arriva' suggested that another bus was coming. Which, to be fair, it was. The only problem was that it wasn't going to Pacentro either, and neither was the third one that showed up.

At 10:40 am, a bus pulled up with the word 'Pacentro' displayed above its windshield. I figured this was a good sign, as I and a handful of others clambered aboard.

The bus may have arrived late, but to our driver's credit, he did all he could to make up for lost time, attacking the corners of our mountain circuit with all of the voracity and focus of an F1 driver in the final stages of qualifying.

I firmly held on to the top of the seat in front of me and the side of the one next to me (lest I be hurled onto the floor) as we shaved precious seconds from our initial delay.

Twenty minutes later, we arrived, and with a bus timetable folded neatly in my pocket, I confirmed with the driver that the return leg to Sulmona would indeed be leaving from the same spot.

I was wary of getting lost, but there was a striking visual reference point close by, in the shape of a very tall medieval bell tower (which negated the need for a map) as I strolled along Via Castello in search of the village's most notable attraction.

Castles aside, Pacentro is a beautiful village. Its narrow, cobbled laneways are bordered by tall, stone houses with cast-iron balconies. Many boast colorful flower boxes, while one had elaborate Christmas decorations reposing above and on its front door. Curious, given it was May.

I saw a sign as we arrived that read 'Pacentro - La Perla d'Abruzzo.' No argument there. At the same time, another sign recognized that Pacentro was awarded the title of 'Italy's prettiest village' in 2001.

I am just surprised that it has only won it once.

I would have reached the castle in half the time if I hadn't stopped to take so many photographs.

Tiny, narrow laneways, resting in the shadow of massive snowcapped mountains, were something that (except for Scanno and much of Sulmona) I had never seen before.

Come to think of it, not an entirely uncommon sight in this part of the world.

Eventually, I climbed a sturdy metal staircase that wound around the Caldoresco Castello, before I found the castle's entrance.

Two very amiable and cheerful women were seated in the ticket office. One of them was working on an impressive acrylic painting of the castle itself, and I can honestly say the entry fee was the best €2.00 I am ever likely to invest.

I would have happily paid at least ten.

The castle (which dates back to the seventh century) was spectacular.

It is unfair to describe it as a ruin, since much of it remains intact, including an impressive medieval banquet hall that has a raised platform at one end, with a vast array of swords, shields, and weapons adorning its walls.

It's the perfect wedding venue.

The castle's perimeter presents some spectacular views of the valley below and the mountains beyond, while its three imposing towers define the profile of Pacentro itself.

The Tower of the Siege, the Tower of Possession, and the Tower of the King all stand proudly inside the castle walls, giving every indication they will do so for centuries to come.

When I eventually left the confines of the castle, I sat in the Piazza del Popolo for a few minutes, but not before passing a poster and an office (albeit closed) dedicated to Pacentro's most famous and bizarre annual event.

Every September, Pacentro stages a running race along the rugged paths and trails that surround the village.

The race honors an apparition of the Madonna di Loreto, who appeared at the top of the mountain and ran all the way to the town center.

The race is always run on the first Sunday of the month. It starts from a sheer and coarse escarpment on a hillside outside the town, before competitors cross the Vella River, racing up a steep bank of stones and brambles toward the village, and a finish line defined by the Church of the Madonna.

But what sets this race apart from your run-of-the-mill cross-country challenge is that competitors must compete barefoot. A poster promoting the event celebrates a runner nursing a bruised and battered foot (that is bleeding quite freely) and there is nothing to suggest that he even won.

Each year, the winner is carried through the town on the shoulders of an adoring crowd before (I imagine) the entire field is dispatched to the nearest hospital.

I returned to the bus stop a few minutes before 3:25 pm, where I had the opportunity to thank one of the women from the castle ticket office again, as she had driven there herself to collect her daughter, who was one of a dozen or so schoolchildren who spilled off the bus shortly after it arrived.

As it turned out, I was the only passenger on the bus for the entire return journey to Sulmona.

We left on time, and I got to ride in the world's largest taxi, asking the driver to drop me off at the same point where my journey had begun.

Chapter 59

Twin Sisters

I loved Sulmona.
I loved its spectacular landscape, streets, and laneways.
I loved its buildings, monuments, and piazza.

Above all though, I loved its people.

Everyone I met in Sulmona was unfailingly friendly, helpful, and kind. I didn't go into a single shop or business where I didn't leave feeling happier and more cheerful than before I arrived - with one very notable exception.

I had met a very attractive and delightful woman in a particular shop a couple of times. We had chatted at length, laughed, flirted, and even exchanged email addresses.

She told me that she operated the business in partnership with her twin sister, and when I remarked one day that it would be very embarrassing if I was ever to engage in a playful conversation with her twin, she assured me that the two of them were not identical and that her sister was 'a fatty.'

I returned to the shop one morning armed with a list of ristoranti, trattorie, e pizzerie and was surprised to see Fatty standing behind the counter, as my friend had assured me that she always worked the morning shift before her sister took over in the afternoon.

Undeterred, I confessed that I was hoping to speak with her twin before my friend emerged from the back of the store.

Not thinking for a moment that her sister would have a problem with it, I cheerfully asked if she might like to have dinner with me one evening at a restaurant of her choosing.

She looked at me as if I had just told her she had a terminal illness.

All of the color drained from her face, as she stumbled over the words, "No, that's impossible. I have to work. I'm sorry."

None of it rang the least bit true until I glanced across at Fatty, who looked like she wanted to kill me.

All of a sudden, pennies were dropping from everywhere, and I was able to crack the 'twin sister code' for the first time.

Thinking that perhaps 'twin sister,' is an expression that people of a particular persuasion are inclined to use in strict Catholic countries, I swallowed my pride, and quietly made my way out of the store.

Feeling embarrassed, foolish, and depressed, I made a detour past the supermarket at the top of il Corso Ovidio, before getting caught in a thunderstorm on the way home.

Sometimes, you just back the wrong horse.

Chapter 60

Il Vecchio Muro

I did go out to dinner to celebrate my last night in Sulmona, however.

Having asked my B&B host Paolo to narrow down the list of options at my disposal, I settled on a trattoria by the name of:

Il Vecchio Muro   The Old Wall

Strictly speaking, I thought it should be Il Muro Vecchio, with the adjective placed after the noun.

However, I did recall (from an earlier lesson) that putting the adjective before the noun is often okay in order to emphasize it.

In this case, perhaps the wall in question was positively ancient, but it's not as if I was about to show up and point out they had made a mistake.

The trattoria was scheduled to open at 7:30 pm, and I took the unrealistic precaution of emailing them the previous day to reserve a table for one.

Il Vecchio Muro was located in a street that led away and down from the piazza. I entered via a rustic timber gate and along a narrow path that ran alongside an old stone wall, generously adorned with rusty metal farming implements and tools.

There was an outdoor dining area to my right and the trattoria proper to my left.

I opened the door shortly after 7:30 pm to see two camerieri leaning on a counter, behind which was a large wood-fired pizza oven.

I never received a reply to my email and confirmed (as best I could in Italian) that I had sent one when one of the two camerieri nodded as if to say, 'So, that was you then.'

I was the only person in la trattoria at this stage and outnumbered at least five to one by staff members that I could actually see.

In hindsight, the email was a bit excessive.

I was led to a small table (that was itself set against an old stone wall) and presented with a menu.

The first two pages listed several dishes under the heading 'Primo piatto.'

Subsequent pages listed still more dishes under the heading 'Secondo piatto', and there was no shortage of options and choices after that, before we even reached the 'Dolce' page.

Given the layout of the menu, I thought it would be downright rude of me to order just one course, so I settled on a pasta dish of spaghetti with a cheese and black pepper sauce, followed by a pizza with tomato, basil, and mozzarella.

All this would be washed down with a glass of local red wine.

Not long after placing my order, 'una cameriera' walked past, dropping a small brown paper bag on my table.

It looked like the sort of packed lunch I might take to school, and sure enough, it contained several slices of delicious sourdough bread.

A few more people arrived soon after, and two families had been seated by the time my primo piatto was placed on the table in front of me.

The serving of my pasta dish was much larger than I had expected and presented within a crudely shaped vessel of (I think) dried cheese. This was, in turn, placed within a much larger ceramic bowl.

Whatever it looked like, it was the most delicious pasta dish I had ever eaten.

The spaghetti was indeed 'al dente' (much firmer than I am used to cooking for myself) and the combination of a simple cheese sauce with flecks of black pepper was a marriage made in heaven.

My only concern (as I devoured every last morsel) was that I still had a pizza to come and very little room to accommodate it.

If I had the opportunity, I would have called time then and there, enjoyed my wine, paid il conto, and happily wandered off home.

Make no mistake, if I am hungry, I can eat a horse and chase the rider, but I have clearly got nothing on the Italians and their capacity to put food away.

I would have happily waited at least an hour for that pizza to arrive.

When it did (a few minutes later) it looked delicious, spectacular, and from my appetite's perspective, practically impossible.

After a sip of wine and a small drink of water, I did my best to focus on the task at hand.

I could see two pizza chefs standing in front of the oven ahead of me, and having no desire to disgrace myself or upset them, I made my first few forays with a knife and fork.

It was a struggle from the outset.

I managed to make slow and steady progress however, aided by the odd sip of wine and the occasional drink of water, while needless to say, the bread stayed in the bag.

Eventually (somehow) I managed to eat the whole thing, and I can honestly say I had never felt so full.

It's a shame because I wasn't being the least bit fair to what was a very cozy and friendly establishment, one that had presented me with two delicious offerings that, in hindsight, should have been consumed on different days, probably a week apart.

Il cameriere collected my plate and returned soon after, asking me if there was anything else that I might like.

A lift home came to mind, but I replied, "No, grazie."

Even the tiniest sip of water struggled to find any room in my stomach, as I sat in my seat contemplating the fact that I had a short uphill walk to il Corso Ovidio, before a downhill stretch of cobblestone that may yet allow me to roll the rest of the way.

Thinking that my best strategy was to stand up and get moving, I asked for il conto, presented my debit card at the cash register, and made my way outside.

I hadn't walked far before my strategy was already proving a failure. It was difficult enough to remain upright, let alone move, and dealing with the uphill section of road leading to the piazza, was like tackling one of the steeper climbs on the Giro d'Italia.

Having finally reached the summit, I glanced to my left at what was by now a very familiar avenue and slowly set about reaching the veritable oasis of Via Paolina.

I ticked off some of the shops and businesses in il corso as I went (enacting the entire exercise in slow motion) before I caught sight of the Annunziata Church Complex that was more or less opposite my apartment.

The only disappointment I felt was that the process of walking wasn't making the slightest difference to my body's capacity to settle and digest the meal, as I continued to feel just as uncomfortably full as I had when sitting in Il Vecchio Muro.

I was, however, just a few steps from my apartment, and after fumbling with a couple of keys, I was soon inside.

I felt sure I would fall asleep within seconds, but I lay in bed for what seemed like an hour, nursing a discomfort in my midriff that I hadn't endured since my hernia operation.

I was finally horizontal however, and not lying in the street, which in and of itself was something of a triumph.

Thinking that I probably wouldn't have to eat anything for the next three days, I could finally relax and eventually drift off to sleep, bestowing upon my digestive system the arduous task of processing the job at hand.

Chapter 61

Bari Vecchia

When researching my trip to Italy, I settled upon two regional destinations: Abruzzo and Puglia, which, as far as I could tell, would present two vastly different landscapes: Abruzzo, the mountains, and Puglia, the sea.

I further refined my search and narrowed things down to Sulmona and Bari, or Bari Vecchia, to be precise.

Bari Vecchia is the original township that has housed fishermen and their families for centuries, as opposed to Bari itself, a new and much larger section of the town, developed on the other side of il Corso Vittorio Emanuele II, which will probably attract thousands of tourists and their families for generations to come.

Bari's modern high-rise apartments and tree-lined shopping malls contrast Bari Vecchia's narrow, winding laneways and wonderful old-stone buildings.

As if to reinforce the cultural and historical divide, the bottom corner of Bari Vecchia houses the picturesque and spacious Piazza IV Novembre.

By comparison, and directly opposite, Bari has a McDonald's.

Bari gives the impression that the forces of rampant commercialism have massed along the border, just waiting for the opportunity to invade.

My two-week lodging was an apartment hosted by a woman named Claudia. She was kind enough to meet me in the nearby Piazza San Pietro (as that was as close as the taxi I had taken from the station could get) and escort me to the narrowest and tallest residential building I had ever seen, but one I daresay is typical of Bari Vecchia.

The apartment was undoubtedly secure, with two separate front doors, and given I had to lock each one with a different key as I left each day, it seemed highly unlikely that I would ever lock myself out.

That was a comfort.

Directly inside was a small kitchen that bordered a bathroom and shower.

Immediately ahead of the two front doors was an almost vertical marble staircase. That led to a lounge room before a second flight of stairs (also marble and just as steep) led to a bedroom, with a third flight leading to a laundry and a tiny cast-iron balcony.

Claudia explained that it was important to keep the door to the upstairs balcony locked, as it wasn't particularly difficult, for a relatively nimble individual, to climb across from any number of neighboring buildings onto the balcony itself, and thus into the laundry and rooms below.

The building's most unique feature, however, was a bathroom that was 'accessed' from the third-level bedroom. The facilities were wedged underneath the stairs that led to the laundry and at the top of the stairs leading into the bedroom itself.

While I salute the effort in trying to make use of what little space there was, it was a perilous exercise to entertain at any time of the day, let alone in the middle of the night.

Accessing the bathroom meant straddling the top two steps of the stairwell and making one significant stride into the space itself (always using the door frame as leverage) while being careful not to hit my head on the ceiling.

The safest and most sensible solution became the elimination of fluid intake from late afternoon.

I had timed my visit to Bari Vecchia to coincide with the town's biggest annual event, a three-day religious festival called, 'La Festa di San Nicola,' which celebrates the return of the remains of Saint Nicholas (aka Santa Claus) from Turkey in 1087.

I have no idea what his remains were doing there in the first place, but it was certainly no secret that the festival was on, as the town was absolutely heaving with people when I arrived.

I walked along the foreshore, where a street market had been set up, just as a team of people were erecting panels of security fencing to protect a street parade scheduled for that evening.

All of the usual suspects were among the market stalls. There were several food trucks, with others selling handbags, T-shirts, jewelry, and, in what was a first for me, vacuum cleaners.

The festival would start that evening with a service in the Basilica di San Nicola at 6:30 pm. This would be followed by a street parade ending at the same venue around midnight.

I was under the impression that a team of people would carry a statue of San Nicola through the streets, and when I wandered into the basilica, just before the service commenced, I could see such a statue reposing to the left of the altar. Thinking that I had secured an excellent spot to see the parade begin, I stood at the back of the church, watching an entire ninety-minute service unfold, before realizing that said statue wasn't going anywhere.

I then went off in search of its parade version, walking along the crowded market-stalled foreshore, where even more people had assembled than before, peering into the distance and hoping to catch sight of San Nicola's statue being carried amid the gathered hordes.

Just for a moment, I thought I had spotted it. But my excitement soon turned to disappointment, when I realized that what I had seen was not in fact an icon of the celebrated saint himself, but a Super Mario balloon.

I then changed my approach and decided to secure a position outside the basilica and wait for the parade to reach me.

This strategy proved more viable, as I sat on a raised stone balustrade (positioned at the edge of the street) that ran alongside the basilica and formed the penultimate section of the parade route.

I was able to pass the time chatting with a woman who was born in Bari, but who now lives in Torino and goes by the name of (would you believe?) Cinthia.

Moments before, she had scolded some fellow for placing a glass bottle on the ground behind the stone border, rather than keeping it in his backpack and disposing of it (properly) later.

"Ben fatto," I told her, recycling a phrase that la professoressa had been kind enough to write on il mio compito once or twice.

Eventually, the parade turned the corner, and it soon became clear that the procession was a much grander, longer, and noisier affair than I had ever imagined.

I lost count of the people involved, but it had to number several hundred.

Many wore period costumes representing Bari, its neighboring towns and regions, differing periods of history, and (rather sportingly) invading forces such as the Normans.

At the head of the procession was a troop of drummers, all wearing matching tunics that looked to display a castle fortress or tower. Their presence was no secret, as they introduced the rest of the parade by belting out the most wonderful if slightly deafening, drum melodies.

Costumed colleagues followed in a sequence that stretched for hundreds of yards. Some blew trumpets that were five feet long, while others performed choreographed routines where they would toss flags (attached to poles) high in the air, catching them as they descended.

The crowning glory of the parade saw dozens of men dragging a replica fifty-foot wooden sailing boat.

The boat was carrying two people who were holding a large portrait of San Nicola himself.

This was intended to re-enact the moment when the saint's remains were repatriated (don't ever say stolen) from Turkey and sailed across the Adriatic to Bari, where they now reside in the Basilica di San Nicola, under the protection of the Catholic Church.

The portrait was carried from the ship and into the basilica, which finally ended proceedings before a large crowd began to disperse.

It was close to 1:00 am by now, and we could all return home while looking forward to the San Nicola Celebration Fireworks scheduled for 4:30 am.

Bang on time (pun intended) the fireworks started, and I can honestly say that even though I didn't see them, they certainly didn't sound like any fireworks I had ever heard before.

San Nicola's Celebration Fireworks sounded more like anti-aircraft artillery than anything bright, expansive, and colorful. But perhaps that was the whole idea. The intention may have been to fire a few shots across the bow of any approaching ships with designs on the old saint's bones.

Chapter 62

Enterprising Nonnas

S trolling through the streets of Bari Vecchia can feel like
stepping back in time.

That is until you are jolted back to the present day when
forced to practice the fine art of Vespa dodging.

There are clearly no rules when it comes to the co-habitation
of Vespa and pedestrian, while it is apparently contingent upon
those on foot to be just as agile and nimble as their motorized
cousins.

Having exceptional hearing and eyes in the back of your head
is no disadvantage either.

All the same, it is certainly worth the risk and effort to explore
Bari Vecchia's fascinating landscape.

For one thing, there are a couple of very narrow laneways,
where it is possible to see a particular pasta being made, to receive
some detailed instruction as to how you can make it yourself, and
to buy bags of the stuff.

These laneways don't house any factory or workshop, mind
you. They are home to a handful of dedicated and enterprising
older women, who sit outside their homes with timber boards
resting on their laps, folding, cutting, and shaping Puglia's signature
pasta - 'Orecchiette.'

Orecchiette means 'small ears,' which reflects the pasta's unique shape.

It is also made with semolina flour and water, no eggs.

Traditional Puglian recipes and dishes, such as Orecchiette, evolved more from economic necessity, rather than any culinary experimentation, as local people used whatever ingredients were available to them.

The concept became known as Cucina Povera or food for the poor.

While vegetables and seafood are often included, meat rarely features.

When making Orecchiette, the pasta dough is molded into finger-width 'snakes' before being cut into bite-sized pieces and shaped by hand.

The nonnas of Bari Vecchia make the entire process look deceptively simple.

Generations of experience and expertise have enabled them to construct each delicious morsel so that its center is slightly thinner than its rim, giving the pasta its distinctive chewy texture.

It is fascinating to see Orecchiette being made and relatively inexpensive to buy.

€6.00 will buy a large bag of a fresh homemade product that could comfortably feed four people, and in my experience it goes very well with a simple Ragu or tomato-based sauce.

Seeing these wonderful women hard at work, meticulously shaping each 'ear' in less than a second, makes for a curious contrast as tourists hover and watch while eating ice creams.

Bari Vecchia's pasta nonnas are an anachronistic breed, contrasting sharply with the town's tacky souvenir shops, all of which present the usual array of printed aprons, dish towels, and fridge magnets, many featuring images of San Nicola himself.

I often wondered what the saint would make of it all.

The same day that I discovered it, I purchased and carried a large bag of Orecchiette around the nearby Castello Svevo Normanno.

The castle is an imposing structure, initially built in 1132 by the Norman King Roger II.

However, King William I of Sicily took exception to it and his forces destroyed the fortress in 1156 before it was rebuilt in 1233 by those loyal to the Holy Roman Emperor Frederick II.

Today, the castle is surrounded by a moat on three sides, bordering the sea on a fourth.

As a medieval fortress, it's a bit of a letdown, given it doesn't display any weapons or shields.

These days, the castle is used mainly for art and sculpture exhibitions. Still, it houses a fascinating collection of ancient Greek artifacts and relics that date back to the eighth century BC. Clear and lasting proof, that the Greeks sailed across the Ionian Sea and established a string of settlements along the Puglian coast.

That was until the Romans arrived and sorted them out in 272 BC.

With dinner in hand, on my way home, I called into a local corner store that, although relatively small, seemed to stock everything I was ever likely to need to prepare a simple and healthy colazione for myself each day.

The store was owned and managed by a very cheerful woman, who seemed only too happy to indulge my clumsy Italian, and the scene of my most significant language assimilation success to date when I made a remark (in Italian) that made her, a man I am pretty sure was her husband, and two other people laugh out loud.

Two female customers had inquired about the various flavors of gelato that the store stocked, and after a quick trip 'out the back,' said husband returned with three large tubs of ice cream, all possessed of different flavor combinations.

He had just presented the characteristics of each tub to the two women when I turned to them both and remarked, "Voglio venire alla tua casa."

The two women laughed, while my friend and her husband joined in.

I had, of course, just suggested, "I want to come to your house."

As delighted as I was that I could present such a consideration in Italian and make a small group of people laugh, I just wish they had realized that I was in fact being quite serious.

No invitation was forthcoming, however, so I returned to 'Fortress Bari,' wrestled with the front door locks, and dropped my provisions off in the kitchen.

Chapter 63

Street Food

According to my Italy travel guide, Bari Vecchia is renowned for the range, diversity, and quality of its street food.

As inviting as it was to sit at a table outside one of the town's many restaurants, I was anxious to sample some of the Bari Vecchia's famous seafood, amid the tangle of narrow laneways I had so enjoyed navigating for the past week.

I had spotted one specialist and tiny, seafood outlet a couple of days before.

It was little more than a doorway that included a cash register, a very small kitchen, and a stack of cardboard containers that would (no doubt) house various elements of Frutti di Mare.

I felt sure I would wander past the same enterprise again before long, and sure enough, I did, early one afternoon.

This time, I studied a poster that presented various photographs, together with descriptions, of each dish on offer.

I was busily rehearsing my order, when the chef came outside to announce, "We will not be taking any more orders for the next ten minutes!"

I thought I must have arrived at a particularly busy time, and the kitchen had a backlog of orders to clear. Or perhaps he and his colleague were in the process of accepting a delivery, but as it turned out, said chef just wanted to sit outside for a few minutes and smoke a cigarette.

After waiting patiently for the kitchen to get up and running again, I presented my order to a rather indifferent and unhappy-looking woman, who gave me the impression that she had been working there for far too long.

Nonetheless, I presented an order in my very best and most enthusiastic Italian.

She responded by staring at me, while not registering the slightest interest.

Shaking her head from side to side, she said nothing but tapped at a copy of the menu poster (attached to the counter) with a long painted fingernail.

Her directive was perfectly clear.

'Just shut up and point at the one you want.'

I did just that, and having spotted a portable card payment processor, sitting next to the cash register, I asked her, "Posso pagare con una carta?"

Apparently, this wasn't possible, as she had already started printing 'lo scontrino,' so I handed over some cash instead.

I was starting to feel a bit uncomfortable by this stage and thought that perhaps I could smooth things over, and repair our somewhat fractured relationship, by suggesting she round up the price of my meal to an even eight euros.

But judging by the amount of change I had just been handed, she already had.

My receipt was numbered and my order defined as 'Quarantadue,' before I spent the next few minutes sitting on a timber bench, reveling in the spectacle of that same woman rifling through the contents of three trash cans in the street.

She was elbow-deep in her third can when I heard 'Smokey the Chef' call out, "Quarantadue."

To her great credit, his colleague immediately returned to her post, collected the order, and handed me my food.

My meal consisted of a dozen deep-fried calamari rings and five or six barbecued shrimps.

The chef had housed everything in one of the shallow cardboard containers, together with a slice of lemon, and a thin wooden skewer that stood upright at its center.

I squeezed the lemon and removed the skewer (thinking a couple of them might have come in handy a few minutes earlier during the trash inspection) before devouring a portion of calamari.

That was when I first realized that the shrimp had been cooked whole. Heads, shells, tails, and legs were all still present.

I was, of course, tasked with amputating and unwrapping them (resting the box on my lap) while doing my best not to drop everything in the street.

I never actually looked up to check, but I am willing to bet that misery guts herself was just waiting for it to happen.

The process I chose to deploy was to eat two portions of calamari before tackling each shrimp.

I rested the skewer in the hinge of the box, using the lid to house the remnants of each creature.

The idea was to gently press each side of the box against my lap with the inside of my wrists. That would more or less free up each hand.

The heads were easy enough to deal with, the legs less so, while the main challenge was identifying and removing the shells from the animal's torso.

I could have eaten all of the calamari first. That would have minimized the damage in the event of a major seafood spill. But I was anxious to convey the impression that I wasn't the least bit daunted by the entire exercise.

Even though I had to sacrifice a tiny portion of meat, just above the tail, eating my first shrimp was a success.

I then tackled shrimp number two, having rewarded myself with a couple of calamari rings.

I briefly flirted with the idea of using my skewer to remove the shells. However, I soon dispensed with that notion and reverted to an entirely manual approach.

To this day, I don't know what that skewer was doing there in the first place, but everyone got one.

Before long, all of the calamari had been consumed, and there was just one shrimp left.

I was determined to complete the exercise successfully, as I slowly and methodically deployed the same amputation and de-shelling procedure that had served me so well in the past, and in less than a minute, the entire process was complete.

Suffice it to say, my fingers were a slippery, greasy mess, but I managed to close the lid on the box, with all of the shrimp detritus contained therein, before licking each digit clean in the most calm, relaxed, and dignified manner possible.

I then sat on the bench for a few minutes, celebrating my success, before standing up and slowly walking toward the three trash cans that were reposing to the left of the doorway.

I shoved the entire box in one, brushed my hands, more or less, clean, and casually wandered up the street.

Chapter 64

Crossing the Divide

The contrast between Bari Vecchia and Bari itself could not be more striking.

With the exception of a few shops (located outside of the old city walls) on the southern side of il Corso Vittorio Emanuele II, I was never able to detect the slightest intrusion of modern-day commercialism or development anywhere near or within Bari Vecchia itself.

Whoever is responsible for maintaining this absolute, and clearly very strict policy, should be congratulated.

The nature, configuration, and character of Bari Vecchia's historic buildings, laneways, and streets are simply untouchable, and rightly so.

Standing on either side of the street that borders Bari Vecchia and Bari can feel like peering over the Berlin Wall, and catching a glimpse of how the others live, needless to say, without the border guards, razor wire, and semi-automatic weapons.

I made my first foray across the divide when I needed to extend my Italian SIM card and find an ATM.

I found a TIM retail outlet easily enough and explained that I needed to extend my cell phone's Internet connectivity for another three weeks.

It was yet another triumph for rudimentary language skills and elaborate gestures.

All the same, I still couldn't be sure that I hadn't already gifted the TIM Corporation every asset I owned, via the medium of the four-page agreement I had signed in Pescara.

Bari itself is a very modern, vibrant, and affluent town. It is littered with boutiques, shoe shops, restaurants, and cafés.

It has a train station, an international airport, a seaport that links it to Greece, Albania, and Croatia, and any number of clearly defined pedestrian crossings that the vast majority of motorists pay absolutely no attention to whatsoever.

To this day, I am convinced that Italian Traffic Laws list adherence to stopping at pedestrian crossings under a section headed, 'Optional.'

Just as safely negotiating the narrow laneways of Bari Vecchia requires a significant degree of Vespa awareness, assuming that cars will stop as you approach, or are in the process of using, a pedestrian crossing in Bari is fanciful.

Time and again, I would use a designated crossing (one that was clearly marked and signposted) only to find myself standing in the middle of the road, weaving a path through the oncoming traffic, while feeling genuinely surprised, and grateful when a car actually did stop.

Having survived a few close encounters, I walked to the railway station and wandered inside to study the lay of the land when it came to purchasing tickets.

I had printed my train ticket to Rome before I had left the States, but I was planning a day trip to Polignano a Mare and wanted to weigh up the options of queuing, using a ticket machine, or the Trenitalia website.

There was quite a long queue at the ticket office, and I didn't bother to check the machines, as I didn't think for a moment that any instructions would be presented in English, before deciding that the website was my best option.

It was only a short journey, I think thirty-five minutes, and there had to be a good chance that no one would check my ticket anyway.

I left the station and crossed a few streets at traffic light intersections, some of which featured a ten-second countdown clock for pedestrians. This meant that anyone could be halfway across the street, only to discover they were fair game for any passing motorist in three or four seconds' time.

Eventually, I noticed a very friendly-looking trattoria that was doing a brisk lunchtime trade.

I secured a table on the street, next to a border of plant boxes, before gifting my table's second seat to three women, who appeared to be taking a break from a major shopping expedition.

They immediately buried the chair beneath any number of bags (each branded with some of Bari's better boutiques) and occupied the table next to mine.

I sat quietly for a few minutes, enjoying the fact that a border of tall green shrubs sheltered me from much of the streetscape, and after briefly perusing a menu, I ordered, "Una bottiglia d'acqua minerale frizzante, e una pizza Bufalotta."

The pizza arrived with a simple tomato base, topped with buffalo mozzarella and basil.

It was presented as a single serving on a large flat platter.

This allowed me to cut it into four equal sections, folding each one in half (lengthways) and eating it with my hands, just as our native Italian instructor Franco had demonstrated over lunch at a pizzeria in Greenpoint, shortly before I left.

In so doing, I hoped that I might be perceived as a cut above the average tourist by my fellow diners, the neighboring shopaholics, and the young cameriera.

But to be honest, I don't think anyone really cared that much.

Chapter 65

Polignano a Mare

It was quite a long walk to the Bari Centrale railway station, as I chose to navigate the outskirts of Bari Vecchia, before following the same tree-lined street I had strolled down the previous day, the one with the McDonald's on the corner.

The idea was to turn right at the same bland, gray apartment building with the crude black graffiti scrawled on a wall at its base, as having already mapped out this same course, I knew that street would lead to the station.

The problem was that just about every corner had a bland, gray apartment building with crude black graffiti scrawled on a wall at its base, and needless to say, they couldn't all lead to the station.

Happily, I had given myself enough time to get slightly lost before standing in the ticket queue at the station.

However, it still ended up being quite a close-run thing.

I had lost an argument with the Trenitalia website the previous day when it continued to insist that I had entered the date of my return journey incorrectly.

For the record, I was selecting a date from the website's own calendar, while shouting a few choice words at the screen of my cell phone, which curiously didn't make the slightest difference.

I arrived at the station fifteen minutes before my train was due to depart, spending much of that time staring daggers into the backs of the people ahead of me in the queue, before I reached the ticket window and was finally given the opportunity to secure my passage.

The ticket seller then listed what sounded like various return timetable options, that, having previously made a careful note of myself, I tried to confirm in Italian.

The original confusion had arisen from the fact that she was actually speaking English.

With two printed tickets, I made my way to platform 8, where a train already crowded with passengers was standing and scheduled to leave in a few minutes.

I walked along the platform to the first carriage and stepped on board, hoping to find a seat.

Five or six people were standing just inside the doorway, and as I turned to my right, I could see a young man occupying a single seat while his bag and jacket were lying across another two.

I felt no compulsion whatsoever to extend him the courtesy of speaking Italian and stood next to the two seats in question, pointing at his belongings, and saying sternly, "Do you mind?!"

He picked up his jacket and bag, as if I had just made the most demanding imposition of him, and dropped them on a single seat.

I sat down, and soon after, another young fellow arrived on the scene, pointing at the same elements, asking, "Posso?"

I replied enthusiastically, "Si, certo!" and ushered him into the seat, as our friend gathered his things and nursed them in his lap.

Anxious not to miss my stop, I had written a sequence of stations that the train was scheduled to call at before Polignano a Mare on a sheet of paper.

Another viable strategy could have been to get off the train when just about everyone else did.

Once we arrived, the train doors opened, and about a thousand people spilled onto the platform.

Various individuals were waiting there; some were presenting colorful brochures, promoting any number of sightseeing options, while a handful of tricycle tour riders were stalking the crowd as it filed past, like a sloth of grizzly bears feasting on a run of salmon making its way upstream to spawn.

Polignano a Mare is, needless to say, a popular day trip destination that essentially has one unique, significant, and spectacular feature.

Its original village, which probably comprises less than a hundred houses, is built around, and quite literally on top of a sheer, rocky cliff face that envelops a small bay, eroded by the ocean's waves for millennia.

It is an extraordinary sight.

It's not just the tall stone dwellings that extend upward from the cliff itself, but the fact that hundreds of locals are happy to swim in the bay and lie on its coarsely pebbled beach, in full view of a few thousand gawking tourists taking photos on their cell phones.

I wandered across the top of the cliff, impressed with the local authority's reluctance to erect anything so much as a sign, let alone a barrier, that might deter someone from wandering too close to the edge and enjoying a sheer three-hundred-foot drop into the water or onto the rocks below.

Of all the sights and sounds of the town, it's certainly hard to miss an imposing, elevated, ten-foot-tall, bronze statue of Domenico Modugno, standing with his arms outstretched, on top of a cliff.

Don't worry. I had never heard of him either, but he wrote and performed the hugely popular song 'Nel Blu, Dipinto di Blu,' which most of us know as 'Volare.'

A song that has, to date, been translated into twenty different languages.

Born in Polignano a Mare, Modugno won the San Remo Music Festival, Italy's most famous song contest, four times, and he played his final concert in the town itself, with an audience of 70,000 people, in 1993.

Having strolled down onto the beach, I stopped for lunch and enjoyed a delicious mushroom pizza, appropriately defined on the menu as 'deliziosa,' before making my way back to the station and Bari Centrale.

I had researched Polignano a Mare on the Internet the day before and found a photograph of the village that insisted every house that sat atop the cliffs and surrounded the bay was a different color.

All the colors of the rainbow were represented, and then some, while no two houses were the same shade.

I can remember thinking, "How on earth did anyone manage to paint all of those houses so many different colors? Let alone maintain them in such pristine condition."

The answer to those questions is that no one ever did and almost certainly never will.

The photograph I saw on the Internet had been altered by someone well versed in the nuances of Photoshop, and who seemed to think that an accurate and realistic representation of the town wasn't impressive enough to attract the interest of any number of visitors.

The houses that top the cliffs, surrounding the bay, are either painted white, with sky-blue window shutters or presented in their original sandstone color.

They are wonderful, stunning, and magnificent exactly as they are.

Whoever was responsible for creating the misleading, full-color abomination I found on the Internet the previous day should switch off their computer and find something better to do.

Chapter 66

Commuting to Rome

O n my way home from the station, I came across a
selection of souvenirs that I actually did consider buying.
A woman had set up one of several stalls in a craft
market being held in the Piazza IV Novembre.

Among other things, she sold handmade and hand-painted
wooden fridge magnets. A selection of which were shaped like the
typical stone houses of Puglia and Abruzzo, complete with flower
boxes and clothes hung outside to dry.

What made her magnets all the more interesting was that the
'clothes' were small pieces of fabric attached to a thin strip of wire
suspended from two tiny pins inserted at either side of the 'house.'

Doors and window shutters presented various bright colors,
and the whole concept was a world away from the molded plastic
muck that was so freely available in the town's tourist trap souvenir
shops.

The woman spoke no English, but I managed to communicate
that I thought her fridge magnets were, "bellisimi e veri."

'Veri,' meaning true, was the best I could come up with in
place of the word, 'authentic.'

In any case, a couple of her creations would be coming home with me.

Two days later, I had a train to catch, and my B&B host Claudia was kind enough to book me a taxi.

I had managed to walk to Bari Centrale before my day trip to Polignano a Mare, but that was without carrying a backpack and dragging a suitcase, and I didn't particularly fancy boarding a train to Rome already exhausted.

Besides, walking would have denied me the opportunity to appreciate the streetscape of Bari from a motorist's perspective.

Here are a few things we can add to the optional section of the Italian Traffic Laws: Red lights, turn signals, and patience.

My driver was a friendly, cheerful, and outgoing fellow. I was flattered that he continued to address me as 'my friend,' but concerned that he would weave his vehicle in and out of the traffic, often leaning on the horn, while shouting at anyone who dared to stop at a designated crossing and allow any pedestrians to pass.

A couple of times, I was tempted to ask, "Why are you sounding your horn? Do you want that car to simply run those people over?"

But fearing the answer may in fact be, "Yes," I let it slide.

In the end, I decided to treat the entire exercise as an expensive carnival ride, while ensuring the integrity of my seat belt and buckle throughout.

A few near misses, two offensive gestures, and fifteen euros later, we retrieved my bags from the trunk, and I made my way into the station.

I had already printed a ticket for the Bari leg of the Frecciargento service from Lecce to Rome, and made my way to its designated platform.

My reservation was housed in carriage two, which suggested that I should wait at a particular end of the platform lest I get on board, only to find myself having to negotiate a route from one end of the train to the other in search of my seat.

A few questions remained, however.

From which direction would the train be arriving, which way would it be heading, and consequently, at which end of the platform should I be standing?

Suffice it to say, I guessed and got it wrong, which necessitated a mad dash with a suitcase in tow, as carriage two sailed past me toward the far end of the station.

Plenty of people were getting on and off, however, and I was able to get on board in plenty of time.

I found my seat, wedged my suitcase onto an overhead shelf, stowed my backpack, and sat down.

When choosing a seat, several weeks before, I had clearly deployed the same interactive conversation strategy, as when traveling from Milan to Pescara.

I found myself sitting behind a narrow table and directly opposite a balding and bearded gentleman, who was far more interested in the contents of his cell phone than me, and who insisted on chewing gum for the entire journey.

He seemed fiercely intent on giving his jaw a thorough, four-hour, aerobic workout; such was the focus and energy he devoted to the task.

"A chain smoker perhaps," I thought, forced to adopt an alternative fix for the next few hours, as he refused to even acknowledge my presence.

Another well-dressed Trenitalia employee was ushering a cart of refreshments along the aisle, handing out bottles of water and packets of cookies.

The water bottles were relatively small (less than half the size of those on the Frecciarossa) but to be fair, the cookies were more appealing than the chips I had enjoyed en route to Pescara.

I wasn't sure just what cookie options were available to me, so I decided to play it safe and opted to receive the same as my neighbor, saying, "Lo stesso per me per favore."

I quickly demolished my packet and was tempted to steal Chewy's when he went to the restroom, but given he had the option of using his gum, in my hair, as a weapon, I thought better of it.

We suffered a fifteen-minute delay, stuck in the middle of nowhere during a storm before we eventually made our way through the outskirts of Rome.

Chewy was the first to collect his bags and wait by the doors, clearly intent on making a swift exit. This gave considerable weight to my chain smoker theory, but for the most part, I was just grateful for a few minutes of extra legroom.

Chapter 67

Conca d'Oro

My train reached Roma Termini shortly after 5:00 pm, and even though it was a Sunday, the station gave me every impression that I had arrived amid its peak hour commuter carnage.

I dragged my suitcase from the overhead shelf, carried my backpack to the door, and stepped onto the platform to see people rushing in all directions.

My task was to find the Metro, buy a ticket, and catch a train to Conca d'Oro.

All of which proved a rather complicated and protracted exercise.

Several signs boasted of new restroom facilities in the station, but there was no indication as to where those facilities were actually located.

In fact, I couldn't make much sense of any of the signs that were directing me anywhere.

I did, however, stumble across an information desk, behind which sat a rather exhausted, and largely uninterested woman.

"Buonasera, signora," I chirped, asking, "Dov'è il Metro?"

She looked at me as if to say, "Seriously?" then pointed downward, with an index finger generously elongated by a painted pink fingernail.

Ask a stupid question.

While searching for an escalator that would transport me underground, I spotted one of the tremendous new restrooms the station had been boasting about.

Unsurprisingly, it cost one euro to use. It had a coin-operated mechanical turnstile, with no cleaner wearing a bright green uniform collecting money and stamping the date on tickets.

I didn't have any change, and I decided to focus my efforts on finding the Metro instead.

Several signs suggested it was located beneath the station concourse, but none indicated a point of access.

I watched a few thousand people move to and fro and walked in the direction that the majority seemed to be heading before I eventually found a couple of escalators beneath a circular sign that had a white 'M' silhouetted against a red background.

I descended, dragging my suitcase into the station, while following the signs directing me towards, 'i treni.'

There was nowhere to buy a ticket from a human being, only a bank of ticket machines with a long queue.

My earlier Internet research had suggested that I needed to buy a ticket for €1.50. This would be valid for a journey of up to one hundred minutes, although the machines quoted seventy-five.

Some machines were card payment only, while others were coin-operated.

I stood back, watching the process unfold for a few minutes, curious that no one was using the card payment machines.

Thinking there would be less pressure from an encroaching queue of locals and experienced tourists, with the card machines, I stepped up, selected a single ticket option, and tried to pay with my debit card.

Nothing happened.

I tried again and then tried an adjoining machine, which delivered a similar result.

"They're broken," I heard a very kind voice say.

It belonged to a Portuguese woman who was only too happy to agree when I asked her to help me, and before long, despite having no coins and only a €5.00 note, I had a single journey Metro ticket and €3.50 in change.

I watched other travelers insert their tickets into machines that granted them access to the platforms and followed suit, before studying a diagram, mounted on a wall, that listed all of the stations on the Rome Metro's Linea B.

To reach Conca d'Oro, I needed to take a train destined for Junio. This was important as two branches of the same line divided at Bologna (the station, not the city) with the other branch terminating at Rebibbia.

The first two trains that stopped at the platform were bound for Rebibbia, but the third was destined for Junio, so I got on board.

The atmosphere aboard the Rome Metro proved just as dire and impersonal as the New York Subway, and I sat quietly ticking off each station until we reached Conca d'Oro.

I was booked to stay one night at the Hotel Aniane and emerged above ground into what I daresay is one of Rome's less attractive neighborhoods.

There weren't many shops or businesses to speak of, just a couple of fast food outlets and small groups of men hanging around street corners.

I didn't want to wander about, much less get lost, so I used my cell phone's GPS function to find my hotel.

I passed any number of dilapidated buildings, walking along a fractured asphalt pavement, before I eventually veered to the left and found what appeared to be an immaculate, modern building that was entirely at odds with its surroundings.

It housed the Hotel Aniane.

Relieved, I entered through an automatic sliding glass door to be greeted by a cheerful fellow and his female colleague.

I explained that I had reserved, 'una stanza' and was directed to an elevator, having been allocated a key card to a room on the third floor.

The room itself housed a single bed. It was clean, tidy, and compact, but perfectly adequate for a one-night stay.

I left my bags inside and went off in search of a place to eat, before stumbling across, of all things, a Bangladeshi restaurant just up the road.

The restaurant was called Tasty, which was enough of an enticement for me.

After devouring a chicken korma, downing a bottle of acqua minerale, and chatting with the owner for a few minutes, I returned to the hotel.

Chapter 68

Swallowed

The next day, I took an elevator to the ground floor of my hotel and wandered into its designated breakfast area.

I am always up for a buffet breakfast, and if I can't eat and drink just about everything in sight, I am almost certain to sample most that's on offer.

I ordered a cappuccino from la cameriera and launched my initial assault with a bowl of muesli, milk, and yogurt. This was followed by a large serving of stone-cold scrambled eggs, which I sought to heat up with four pieces of toast.

This allowed me to explain to some German fellow how the toaster worked after he confessed to giving up on it.

Given his country's propensity for complex engineering, I considered this something of a coup.

All the same, in trying to toast four slices of bread, I could only toast both sides of one piece at any one time and just one side of the other three.

Perhaps the idea was to eat one slice while the other three were still cooking, but it was all rather awkward, and it left me with the impression that toast may not be a particularly popular breakfast fare in Italy.

I then washed down 'due cornetti,' with three glasses of grapefruit juice, before sampling four bread rolls with several slices of ham, cheese, and salami. Finally, I polished off a small custard donut.

I wasn't kidding before about breakfast buffets.

Check-out was 11:00 am, and I had arranged to meet another B&B host at 2:30 pm.

I had plenty of time to return to the Conca d'Oro Metro station, before making my way to a station called Cipro.

Given Cipro was a Rome Metro Linea A destination, I would change trains at Roma Termini.

There was an escalator at street level that descended into the station. It was barricaded with a plastic fence and looked like it hadn't seen active service for months, so I shuffled down the stairs into the heart of Conca d'Oro, where I was pleased to see some people housed inside the ticket office.

I approached, smiled, said, "Buongiorno," and asked for "un biglietto," at which point, in exchange for €1.50, I was presented with a ticket that looked exactly like the one the machine at Roma Termini had spat out for me the previous day.

I dragged my suitcase to the access gates and inserted my ticket, arrow graphic first, with the magnetic strip facing up, just as I had done before.

The machine sucked my ticket in, but rather than spitting it out and opening its gates, as I had anticipated, it decided to ingest the ticket whole and bar me from any platform access.

I returned to the ticket office, while rehearsing my past tense verb conjugations, and said, "La macchina ha mangiato il mio biglietto."

Sadly, my Italian wasn't considered worthy of a verbal reply, or perhaps those in the ticket office didn't find the suggestion that the machine had eaten my ticket very funny.

Instead, I was directed to speak with a couple of maintenance men, housed in a booth on the opposite side of the concourse.

I presented them with the same dilemma, at which point one of the men exited the booth and asked me, "Quale macchina?"

I identified the culprit, and moments later, he had removed the top of the machine, retrieved my ticket, and suggested I try another.

I said, "Grazie mille, signore," and did just that.

The same thing happened.

In fact, it happened three times, with all three platform access machines.

I was left thinking, "Perhaps my ticket was printed on a Monday?" which, oddly enough, it was.

My friend opened the machine again and returned my ticket to me before inserting a key into a disabled access gate. Happily, it opened, and with those in the ticket office smiling and waving cheerfully, I was soon on my way.

After changing trains amid the chaos of Roma Termini, I arrived at Cipro, surfacing in a more vibrant, attractive, and busy neighborhood.

Cars were racing past in all directions, and a handful of market stalls selling clothing, jewelry, and fruit, were set up on the pavement.

Not for the first time, I wasn't entirely sure in which direction to head, so I engaged the GPS app on my cell phone, entered the address details, and followed its instructions.

I had plenty of time up my sleeve, and confident that I was just across the road from my destination, I sat in a small bakery, drinking two bottles of water, while watching customers come and go as they submitted various orders for bread and pastries.

The bakery was doing a roaring trade, for the time I was there anyway, and what struck me throughout was that every single customer greeted the shop owner with a cheerful and respectful 'Buongiorno,' the moment they entered the store.

Thereafter, every transaction was enacted politely and enthusiastically, while the simple process of buying a loaf of bread became something of an event.

The bakery was due to close at 2:00 pm, and anxious not to get in the way, I left at 1:50 pm to wait outside the apartment building for my host to arrive.

A woman named Simona arrived half an hour late.

She represented the owner, and while she may not have owned a watch, she was well-versed in the various nuances and features of the apartment.

We entered a seven-story stone building through a couple of tall, dark timber doors, shuffling past a small cubicle that would usually house a door attendant but didn't today.

We walked up seven or eight steps before we were presented with the sight of a large, dark metal cage that housed the most wonderful old elevator.

There was a single button on the outside of the cage that, when pushed, lit up a small screen that read, 'Occupato.'

A handful of cables and heavy counterweights were housed inside the cage.

They enabled the elevator cell to rise and descend almost silently.

In fact, the most noise it ever made was when someone opened and closed its doors to gain access.

Once a floor had been selected, from a vertical presentation of small black buttons set against a brass control panel, the cell would operate with the most unerring efficiency.

The elevator was a delight to behold, but soon after we reached the third floor, and entered the apartment, things went downhill.

There was a pile of rubbish in the kitchen, dishes in the sink, and the bed hadn't been made, nor the sheets replaced.

I didn't bother to look in the bathroom before Simona glossed over these issues and gave me a brief induction as to where light switches were located, how to open the windows, and where plates, pots, and cutlery were housed.

Having been assured, twice, that a team of cleaners had been summoned, I flopped on the couch and looked up at a large clock on the wall that didn't work.

Chapter 69

Washing Watch

Taking a shower each morning in the apartment was an adventure.

The only way to get any hot water flowing was to turn the tap on full and make use of the fact that the temperature gradually increased, before it became too hot to handle, as any attempt to moderate the temperature thereafter would cut the hot water off altogether, which resulted in a bracing stream of cold water seconds later.

Not what you are looking for with a head full of shampoo.

Suffice it to say, showers were brief, as complaints to the owner only resulted in bland assurances that the hot water was indeed working.

Sadly, at this stage, my Italian vocabulary didn't contain the words, 'regolare' - adjust, 'smette di funzionare' - stops working, and 'maledetto congelamento' - bloody freezing.

Nonetheless, I had a promise to keep and a commitment to honor.

A woman in my Italian class had been born in Rome, but having left Italy as a child, her language skills had faded over the years.

In any case, she was keen to return to the city of her birth one day, and she asked me to help facilitate that process, by tossing a nickel into the pool of the Trevi Fountain on her behalf.

Apparently, tossing a coin into the fountain, over your left shoulder, will ensure you return to Rome one day.

I don't know if the system allows for people to act as a proxy, but given the whole superstition isn't the least bit ancient or mystical (in fact, it originated from a scene in the 1964 film Three Coins in the Fountain) I reckoned we could safely bend the rules a bit.

In order to execute the exercise, I took the Metro from Cipro to Barberini.

Once above ground, I reached an educated guess as to the fountain's location by following a couple of tour groups that were walking down the hill.

I arrived at my destination about five minutes and two thousand tourists later.

The Trevi Fountain is a magnificent, striking landmark, and judging by the number of coins its shallows contained, all of which are collected each day to fund a charity supporting Rome's homeless population, the city's tourism industry doesn't have anything to worry about for the next few years at least.

People were gathered ten deep in front of the fountain, so I made my way over to its far side, where I could secure a degree of access, sufficient for me to fling a coin into its pool while recording the entire event as a video on my cell phone.

The process was enacted, and after taking a few photos, I left the fountain to the masses.

Once I had escaped the crowds and disappeared around the corner, I was able to watch the video I had just produced.

It lasted for little more than a second and was nothing more than a crude, unattractive self-portrait.

I returned to the same spot, at the far edge of the fountain, a few minutes later and tried again, this time with twenty euro cents.

I wasn't about to retrieve the original nickel, as police officers patrol the area with the power to arrest anyone caught trying to collect coins and defraud the charity.

The system may only work with local currency anyway.

This time, the video was a success, and I could present clear and irrefutable evidence that I had honored the undertaking upon my return.

Subsequent research has revealed that tossing one coin into the fountain will ensure that you return to Rome one day while tossing two coins in is supposed to ensure that you will not only return but fall in love.

That's a bit of luck then.

Few things in life are less attractive and stimulating to me than underground railway stations, so I spent the rest of the day on foot, wandering past and toward anything that caught my eye.

I strolled past countless shops, numerous cafés, and several restaurants, to say nothing of some spectacular churches, and imposing monuments, when, for no reason in particular, I turned left along a long, straight stretch of asphalt and pavement.

Before long, at the end of the road and the top of a hill, I could see a massive structure of partial stone ruin.

Rome's Coliseum isn't fenced off and hidden away like some priceless museum exhibit. It stands in the center of the city, with cars, taxis, vespas, and vans encircling it day and night.

Imposing and majestic, it is a beautiful site with an extraordinary history. However, pollution and vibrations, from the nearby Metro, in particular, have taken their toll on the integrity of its structure in recent years.

The Coliseum is breathtaking and just one of so many ancient Roman wonders that visiting them all is seriously hard work.

By complete contrast, I became fascinated and enthralled by the simple and gentle spectacle of several, invariably women, hanging their washing outside their apartment windows.

My apartment may have had the world's worst hot water service, but it did present an uninterrupted view of the residential dwellings opposite and to either side.

Six buildings, all with seven or eight stories, surrounded a rectangular garden courtyard.

Each one housed dozens of apartments, all of which had timber window shutters that opened onto tiny balconies that were, in turn, bordered by cast-iron railings.

Many of these apartments had at least one, often two, washing lines that were little more than thin ropes looped around a simple pulley system, which was attached to a couple of metal brackets and bolted to an exterior wall.

The idea was that whoever was responsible for hanging out the washing could suspend an item of clothing or bed linen on one of the lines. They would then move it along a few feet and attach another item, without having to relocate themselves, or lean out of another window, at any stage.

This process continued until the line was fully extended, and the second line came into play.

The second line was invariably situated further from the exterior wall.

It was pretty hair-raising at times, watching people lean out of their apartment windows, often from a considerable height, draping and pegging their clothes onto thin ropes that they would extend as far as they could before repeating the process.

The heat reflecting from the wall no doubt aided the drying process, and the whole endeavor was entirely practical.

What I enjoyed most, however, was the ever-changing mosaic created by so many people hanging out different items of diverse colors and shapes from various windows every day.

It was a moveable feast that became all the more interesting when rain threatened to fall, as I could sit back and witness who was playing it safe and who was either out for the day or rolling the dice with the elements.

Chapter 70

Trastevere

A few days later, I had arranged to meet and stay with my friend Ashley in Trastevere.

I strolled into the street and tried to hail a taxi when a very kind stranger approached me, explaining that taxis were not allowed to stop by the side of the road in Rome and that I would be much better off walking a short distance to a designated taxi stand.

He gave me a detailed set of directions, clearly indicating that I should walk toward the nearest intersection and make a turn.

He was gesturing to his left, having momentarily forgotten the word, when I offered, "Sinistra?"

"Si, sinistra," he replied.

I cheekily responded, "Lo so meglio di te!" - I know it better than you!

It was a remark that he graciously accepted with all of the good humor that was intended.

As it happened, a taxi was waiting for me when I arrived.

After the driver was kind enough to load my bags into the trunk, I handed him a copy of the address, saying, "Ho bisogno di andare a questo indirizzo per favore."

He nodded, and we were soon on our way.

We hadn't gone far before I discovered two things.

Firstly, my driver was a massive Roma FC fan, and secondly, the Giro d'Italia cycling race was due to finish in Rome the next day, which explained why so many streets had been closed and barricaded to traffic.

He apologized for the fact that we would have to make a couple of detours, to accommodate the Giro route, and he offered me something of a countdown as to our estimated time of arrival in Trastevere.

We had started at twenty minutes and sailed through fifteen.

By the time we had reached ten, he had run two red lights and almost wiped out a middle-aged woman on a pedestrian crossing.

I was searching for the words, in Italian, to say, 'There is no rush. I have got plenty of time.'

But I couldn't be sure that whatever I came up with wouldn't be misinterpreted as, 'Please put your foot down, and take as many outrageous risks as necessary.'

Instead, I could only offer the occasional calm and casual, "Non e problema," while trying to appear as relaxed as possible.

Determined to deliver me to the front door of my apartment building, he plotted a course through several narrow laneways in a manner that suggested any pedestrian would be wise to get out of the way, lest they bounce off the windshield.

"Non e problema," I said, with even more conviction than before, adding, "Posso camminare da qui."

I was, of course, trying to say, 'It's okay. I can walk from here.'

But what I really meant was, 'For God's sake, man, you are going to kill someone!'

He was of course simply doing his best, and he was a very cheerful and friendly soul into the bargain.

All the same, I could have done without the white knuckle element to the whole experience, as I hung on for dear life, choking my seat belt to death in the process.

Eventually, we arrived. I paid my fare, wished Roma FC all the best, and retrieved some keys from a combination lock box. I then opened the door to the apartment, poured myself a drink, and sat on the couch while I waited for my friend.

Trastevere is a former working-class suburb of Rome that in recent years has become a very desirable and trendy part of the city, packed with bars, restaurants, and tourists.

It boasts countless narrow cobblestone streets that, for me, evoked memories of Sulmona and Bari while rendering the process of local navigation practically impossible.

Luckily, Ashley continued to demonstrate the sort of talent that would put a homing pigeon to shame, as he never once failed to get us home after we had spent a day wandering around the city.

We spent two tremendous days walking, eating, and drinking all over Rome and even managed to catch the finish of the Giro d'Italia when we stumbled across one of the city's many barricaded streets at 'just the right time.'

Much like the Tour de France, the Giro, which curiously started this year in Abruzzo, is a grueling and exhausting event that is enacted over more than three weeks.

Not that you would know it, as a fleet of escort and support vehicles raced past, followed by a packed peloton that still seemed to be going at a pretty serious clip from where we were standing.

It was a terrific spectacle that lasted just a few seconds, before we pressed on, ticking off our list of Roman ruins, monuments, and restaurants.

Once we returned to Trastevere, we found a tiny wine bar with a couple of small tables set outside.

We had just ordered two glasses when Ashley suggested I ask the gentleman serving us (almost certainly the owner) if he had any cheese that we could enjoy with our wine.

I didn't think for a moment that he would, but encouraged by my friend and welcoming the opportunity to show off my language skills, I asked, "Scusi signore. Hai del formaggio?"

"Che!" the man practically shouted.

"Apparently not," I said.

Chapter 71

Toscana

In between our exhausting Roman excursions, the two of us spent a day driving to Tuscany, where we met a golfing buddy of Ashley's from the UK, who, like me, was learning Italian but, unlike me, had the good sense to get together with his Italian teacher.

Adam met us in the village of Bettolle and directed us to a magnificent twelfth-century farmhouse that his partner Anna was renovating and converting into a B&B.

Anna was a native Italian, born just north of Venice. She had lived in England for several years and returned to Italy when she (in her own words) 'fell in love with this house.'

Notwithstanding the enormous amount of work and expense involved in its repair and restoration, it wasn't hard to see why.

Casa Ezio Marchi had a charming rural quality, to say nothing of some uniquely historical elements, including an original dry earth wall built by the Lombards, a Germanic tribe of settlers that colonized much of Tuscany in the sixth-century.

The house had been constructed to preserve the integrity of the dry earth wall, a striking and remarkable feature (almost two thousand years old) that had attracted the attention and focused the study of university academics from Florence to Santiago.

Rustic brick partitions, that once defined stables and livestock yards, supported a maze of staircases that led to balconies presenting spectacular views of the Tuscan countryside.

When she wasn't busy correcting my Italian grammar, Anna conducted a tour of the house, pointing out where sheltering cattle had once smoothed the edge from some coarse, cornered brickwork, which now shielded the access to a cellar.

Bedrooms and apartments were located upstairs, where our host had painstakingly restored an original patterned fresco that ran along the top of the walls and bordered the ceiling.

Much of the upstairs sat above a generous lounge with an enormous fireplace and a magnificent, fully appointed kitchen, where we all gathered, before embarking on an excursion of the garden and grounds, with its myriad of olive trees, and bee hives, to say nothing of a swimming pool.

Anna was determined to see the house's original fixtures and fittings restored, and for the renovation to remain as authentic as possible.

She had such a tremendous passion and enthusiasm for the project, that listening to her talk about it was like reading the first few chapters of an adventure romance novel, all the while wanting to skip forward to the end and see how everything turns out.

Tuscany, I learned this day, is named after the Etruscan people, who populated the region for centuries until the ancient Romans arrived and all but wiped out any trace of their existence.

Little is known of the Etruscan civilization and language, with the exception of some recently discovered burial sites and tombs. However, it would appear to have been very sophisticated and intellectually advanced for its time.

Sadly, sophistication and intelligence amounted to little, by way of defense, when pitted against an all-conquering enemy.

We stayed much longer in Bettolle than we had initially planned and had to sacrifice a detour to Orvieto on the way home.

By the same token, the sight of some spectacular hilltop villages was reward enough for spending a few hours in the car.

To say nothing of the task involved in finding somewhere to park the damn thing.

Chapter 72

Taxi to Termini

The next day, Ashley left for the airport early. At the same time, I was presented with the challenge of navigating a path to a nearby taxi stand, before commuting to Roma Termini and eventually, Milan.

I had traversed this same route on the way home a couple of times before, but when it came time to enact it in reverse, I was all at sea.

Happily, I did manage to walk, more or less, in the right direction, through a tangle of Trastevere's narrow, cobbled streets, before I spotted a taxi stand that bordered the same bustling neighborhood where we had been staying for the past few days.

It was, in fact, a different taxi stand altogether, but 'any port in a storm,' as they say.

There was quite a long queue of people, any number of bags, and absolutely no taxis, but secure in the knowledge I had allowed myself plenty of time, I crossed the road and joined the party.

Eventually, the queue started to dwindle, until there was just one older woman ahead of me, who, as it turned out, was 'In attesa di un' amica" - Waiting for a friend.

Working on the assumption that her friend wasn't a taxi driver, I could look forward to loading both my bags and myself into a cab before long.

A few minutes later, a taxi pulled up. I leaned down and spoke to the driver through an open passenger-side window, explaining, "Ho bisogno di andare alla stazione Roma Termini, per favore."

I daresay that including the word, 'stazione' was largely unnecessary, but it never hurts to be sure.

My driver bounced out of his cab, insisting that he load my bags into the trunk before he opened one of the doors and ushered me inside.

He was as typical as any taxi driver I had encountered on my trip, friendly, cheerful, and easily distracted.

We had not long begun our journey before he was watching videos on his cell phone of football supporters singing and chanting, at what appeared to be an airport, before leaning on the horn to attract the attention of another taxi's driver, with whom he enacted a similarly enthusiastic exchange.

He explained, as best as I could understand anyway, that Roma FC and Sevilla, a club from Spain, were playing in the Europa League final in Budapest that evening.

"Quale la tua squadra?" - Which is your team? I said.

This had to be just about the dumbest question anyone had ever asked, since some clown approached the Information Desk at Roma Termini, asking where the underground Metro station was located.

"Roma!" he replied generously, without the slightest hint that he thought I was an idiot.

I tried to resurrect my faltering status in the conversation by wishing him and his team good luck for the final, offering, "In bocca al lupo!"

"Crepi, crepi," he replied.

It was a textbook exchange.

We arrived at the station, and after checking in with a few of his friends at the airport in Budapest, he opened the trunk of his cab and pulled out both of my bags.

He then retrieved his own burgundy and gold-colored Roma FC scarf, waving it joyfully as I paid my fare.

I had arrived at Roma Termini a few times before, but always by train, and this was the first time I could appreciate its exterior before wandering into the station.

It was sleek, modern, and clean. More like an airport than a railway station.

There was a café just inside the main entrance, and I joined a queue of people before ordering, "Un cappuccino e un panino con prosciutto e formaggio, per favore."

It is a great credit to the Italian language that it can make a cup of coffee with a ham and cheese sandwich sound so colorful.

I accepted an offer to have my sandwich toasted, before I delivered my receipt to the coffee section, in exchange for a lukewarm cappuccino.

As disappointing as the coffee was, I managed to secure a seat where I could make out the details listed on the departures board. It confirmed that the Frecciarossa intercity service to Milan was running on time and allocated platform 3.

I decided not to risk a second cappuccino and wandered onto the platform with time to spare. I then strolled toward my designated carriage and climbed aboard.

I had recently amended the date of my ticket and found myself seated in one of four seats on either side of a narrow table, despite the fact, I am pretty sure, that I had selected a single seat on the Trenitalia website.

For once, however, the table strategy worked.

Not because I was seated across from someone who thought I was absolutely fascinating and only too happy to indulge my rudimentary Italian, but because no one sat opposite, or next to me, for the entire journey.

I had expected the Rome to Milan route to be heavily populated with a broad cross-section of the Italian community, together with a handful of tourists.

Perhaps the key was that mine was a 'quiet carriage,' and all the active cell phones, MP3 players, and game consoles had gathered in other parts of the train.

Chapter 73

Milan Again

My train arrived on time at Milano Centrale, and I made my way to the same station exit I had utilized six weeks before, intending to walk to the nearby Hotel Midway, where I had booked a one-night stay.

I then circumnavigated the entire area surrounding the station, retracing my steps more than once, in an exhausting and largely futile exercise sponsored by Google Maps.

The GPS program on my cell phone seemed even more confused than me when it came to locating my hotel.

Each time I refreshed the address details, it all but confessed, 'Well, that didn't work. Let's try over this way.'

I had been assured throughout the process that I was always within four to six minutes of my destination, and it wasn't until my cell phone confirmed it had a three per cent battery life remaining that I finally gave up and asked for directions.

Somewhat ironically, I asked for help at the reception desk of another hotel, where a fellow was kind enough to usher me outside and point across the road to a street where the Midway was one of several hotels that occupied different floors in the same building.

"Grazie mille, signore," I offered, while shaking his hand, genuinely grateful that such a primitive, analog approach had saved the day.

I wandered across the street and found the building in question, which did indeed house several small hotels, each of which had a plaque attached to an exterior wall, next to a sturdy metal gate.

The Midway was located on the fourth floor, and I was able to enter the building, as someone was leaving, to find an elevator.

The doors opened directly opposite a reception desk, where I dropped my bags and waited as a fellow struggled to pay his €5.00 room tax with a cell phone.

Eventually, I checked in and found my room, which was clean, quiet, and perfectly adequate.

The Midway only offered fifteen or so rooms, but it had a designated breakfast area with an espresso machine, which ticked a couple of important boxes.

I relaxed in my room for an hour or so, before venturing outside to find something to eat.

My dining options were limited, as I didn't dare stray too far from the hotel, and I enjoyed what I am reasonably sure was a chicken schnitzel, washed down with a glass of Italy's own Peroni beer.

The following day, I made a serious dent in the breakfast buffet and checked out just short of my 11:00 am deadline before walking to the front of the Milano Centrale station and across the road to the Hotel Bristol, where I had booked a room several weeks before.

The Bristol was a much larger and more established hotel. It had a spacious and luxurious foyer, two elevators, servicing eight floors, and no free-standing, life-size, cardboard cut-out replica of Queen Elizabeth II to be seen.

Apparently, despite my early check-in, I was 'in luck,' and my room was ready.

My room key was attached to a small brass brick, the weight of which suggested I was likely to break a toe if I should drop it, before I made my way to the smallest hotel room in Italy.

The bed was the width of a decent business-class seat, and there was a fold-out wooden chair resting next to a table the size of which we enjoyed on the Frecciarossa.

I left my suitcase hanging over the edge of the bed, took the room key off the brick, which, judging by the ring's integrity, had been done countless times before, and returned to the station.

The Milan Metro presented no great surprises, in that it was also located underground and it was more expensive to use than Rome's.

A single journey in Milan would cost me €2.20, while the same trip in Rome set me back €1.50.

I thought the relevant authority might have invested that additional income in card payment machines and escalators that actually worked, but sadly, no.

Given tickets that would secure a fifteen-minute viewing slot to Da Vinci's Last Supper were booked out for the next six weeks, I decided instead to visit two of Milan's most popular attractions. Namely il Duomo, the city's spectacular landmark Gothic cathedral, and la Galleria di Vittorio Emanuele II, a shopping precinct that houses a handful of hugely expensive designer retail outlets, housed in what I had been assured was a magnificent building.

Emerging above ground at il Duomo station, I was immediately presented with the sight of Milan's signature masterpiece.

Il Duomo took almost six centuries to build, (it was finally completed in 1965, although some claim it remains unfinished) and that from a distance looked like the world's most enormous termite mound, with thousands of tourists scurrying back and forth, in, out, and over its ornate and spectacular structure.

La Galleria di Vittorio Emanuele II was located close by. It did indeed house any number of hugely expensive designer retail outlets, in a shopping mall that comprised two magnificent glazed-roof arcades, crowned by a single and enormous glass dome. Beneath which, countless tourists shuffled about with no apparent intention of doing anything much at all.

I took a few photos and wandered off in search of some souvenir bookmarks for a friend, eventually stumbling upon a dilapidated second-hand bookstall set up on a street corner.

Hundreds of books were housed on a disheveled timber trailer that looked like it had been built in the nineteenth century and drawn there by a team of donkeys. This may have explained the proprietor's absence, as he was probably off somewhere feeding his stock and giving them something to drink.

I was able to browse through titles such as Leo Tolstoy's 'Guerra e Pace,' and any number of second-hand movies on DVD, including 'La Colazione da Tiffany,' and rather appropriately, 'Vacanze Romane,' before I found a cheerful and bustling trattoria for lunch.

Chapter 74

Arrivederci

B reakfast at the Bristol resembled a game of musical chairs. The buffet was excellent, but for a hotel with about a hundred rooms, its designated 'zona colazione' was remarkably small.

I counted about a dozen tables before I secured one next to the bar.

No sooner had I ordered my first cappuccino, than several other people arrived, wandering about in search of a table, often speaking to waiting staff who, while acting genuinely surprised there weren't any, suggested they take a seat at the bar, where they could perch on a stool, sip an espresso, and ready themselves to pounce on my table the moment I stood up.

My dilemma, of course, was how to preserve the integrity of my reservation while I made a trip to the buffet.

If an empty coffee cup should be cleared away in my absence, I was likely to find two overweight Germans occupying my table when I returned.

I decided therefore to make a series of short guerilla-style raids, leaving a not-quite-empty coffee cup and a pair of eyeglasses on the table, before I sat down again with a glass of fruit juice and a couple of bread rolls.

At one point, I took a risk and journeyed to the far end of the buffet. I returned with a plate fairly heaving with scrambled eggs but waiting for any toast to cook was out of the question.

For the record, I did offer to share my table with a couple of people, but they all declined, expressing about as much interest in me as those I sat opposite on the Frecciarossa.

I ate as much as I could, as quickly as I could, leaving the starving hordes to fight over my table, and checked out shortly before 11:00 am, explaining that my flight home was in the evening and that I was hoping to store my bags in the hotel for much of the day.

Happily, this wasn't a problem, as my bags were deposited in a closet, only slightly smaller than my room, before I made my way once again to Milano Centrale.

I took the Metro to San Ambrogio and emerged above ground, asking a woman who owned a newsstand how I could find il Museo Nazionale di Scienza e Tecnologia.

She gave me every indication that this was a question she had answered about a thousand times before. Looking bored and frustrated, she said nothing, but pointed straight ahead and then to the left.

I arrived at the museum having enacted the process of paying for an entry ticket online the previous day.

This ensured I wouldn't have to tackle a queue that didn't exist.

The museum was housed in a disused monastery, and it presented any number of sections and galleries, including a timeline display that featured popular household items and accessories defined by each decade.

I can't tell you how sobering it is to see a rotary phone and a Sony Walkman displayed in a museum.

Its most fascinating gallery, however, was devoted to the great Leonardo Da Vinci.

The museum boasts the world's most extensive collection of Leonardo's original engineering drawings, many of which have since been developed as models.

There is everything from a parachute and a helicopter, to armored fighting vehicles and all manner of for their time, sophisticated weaponry.

The illegitimate son of an Italian nobleman, Leonardo was packed off to Florence at the age of fifteen because he could draw, where, among countless other things, he developed the concept of harnessing solar energy in the sixteenth century.

The man was a genius.

I stayed at the museum for about four hours (only part of which was spent waiting for a toasted salami and cheese focaccia in the garden café) before I returned to the Hotel Bristol, collected my bags, and made my way to Milano Centrale for one last time.

The next train to Malpensa Airport was allocated platform 1, which meant something of a hike to reach the train itself and walk almost its entire length before I found a largely empty carriage.

In a few hours, I would be leaving Italy and longing to return.

Despite dicing with death en route to Scanno and risking a dose of Salmonella poisoning in Bari Vecchia, I had managed to indulge something of my newfound language skills in a country populated by the most kind, friendly, and generous people I had ever met.

Italy has an extraordinary history, a glorious language, and a culture that is the envy of the world.

If my travel guide hadn't been stowed in a suitcase and housed in the fuselage of a passenger plane, I would have spent most of the flight home researching and planning my next trip and book.

For the time being, however, I could be grateful that a friend had offered to pick me up from the airport, and as we walked to his car, I remarked, "On the way home, can we stop off in Little Italy? I fancy a coffee."

Also by Michael Francis:

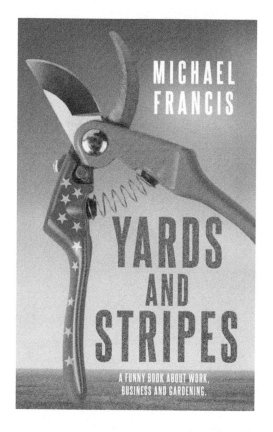

Unlock an inspirational journey of self-discovery in *Yards and Stripes*. The story of an enterprising New Yorker who starts a gardening business in Greenwich, Connecticut, when he doesn't know a weed from a wisteria.

Scan the QR code below to check out the book.

Made in the USA
Monee, IL
05 December 2024

72575041R00154